Came to Believe

Sandra Lund

Dedication

This book is dedicated to my wonderful grown children, Kevin and Kelsey. They have supported, encouraged and loved me through every day of my life.

Prologue

This is my true story. It began in my childhood with me growing up in a dysfunctional household. I had an alcoholic father and a mother in denial – who had an affair as her escape. And it ends with my marriage held hostage by alcoholism, having two children, and my husband committing suicide.

It's about finding love, losing love and questioning life and the choices we all make and why we make them. It's a journey from a fairytale feeling you have when you are 27 and in love; hopeful for a new beginning and brighter future and a struggle to live in and through the years of turmoil due to addiction to alcohol. I don't wish that on anyone.

I write this to share and hope that those who pick this up and read it know there's a beginning and end to the struggle. It's just a matter of how you navigate; use the resources you find or create and the start over that is possible for you alone and/or for your family. Many addicts are able to be reached and have very positive outcomes. Mine did not.

I came to believe I did everything possible to try to save him and end his addiction. I like so many were powerless over alcohol. I alone couldn't stop it; sometimes, it is too late and too out of hand. I've been in Al-Anon, a world-wide organization for over a decade. This has provided me the support needed to cope and help me recover from my husband's effects of alcohol and his death. I still attend meetings and have met some of the most wonderful people all who understand, are mutually supportive and provide a safe harbor to talk about moving on and surviving.

I am so grateful and thankful for my children. They were and are the greatest gift from my marriage to Jeff. Without them I'm not sure I would have survived. Much of this I wrote 15 years ago more for therapy and as my own secret journal. A very few select I confided with and shared a rough draft with. All of them agreed it could be helpful to others as they are alone in the battle themselves or with loved ones. It is raw and many scenarios were left out in efforts to protect my kids who are now adults.

Both my children are fully functioning and happy with their lives and their mates. I pray they aren't terribly haunted by their dad's alcoholism. I am now a senior living in sunny Florida; enjoying life and treasuring my time with my children who I am lucky to have living close to me. I am a watercolors and pen and ink artist, pet sitter, substitute teacher, and beach goer.

Contents

Chapter 1: Growing Up

I don't remember much about growing up beside my parents arguing and slamming doors. My father was a successful stockbroker who entertained clients over lunch with martinis. Still, when he came home after a long work day, he would pick up where he left off, drinking and fighting with my mom.

Some nights my dad worked late, and I could sit at the kitchen counter in peace as my mom cooked dinner, chatting about the neighbors. We grew up in northern New Jersey and vacationed at the Jersey Shore for two weeks most summers. I have fond memories of the beach, the warmth and friendships I made while building sandcastles and playing in the surf. I recall the lingering smell of Coppertone on my salty skin, the sun peeking through my hat, and warming my face.

But even as a child, I learned to keep quiet and disappear when my parents began arguing. My dad would scream until he was blue in the face, and afterward, my mom would plaster on a thin smile and adjust her curls. I learned to pretend things were perfect and not tell a soul. Even as a little girl, I thought that if I let anyone in on my family secrets, all hell would break loose. So, I kept quiet. My dad wasn't a beach person, so he only came on weekends. My mom, brother, sister, and I shared wonderful weeks of no fighting in his absence. I loved seeing my mom glow in her freedom. I loved all the moments my father wasn't present, whether he was working late, golfing, or just sleeping on the couch. I grew up wishing him out of the picture. I came to believe this was normal for every teenage girl in the '60s, and it didn't occur to me that other families were any different.

My mom was an incredible portrait artist before meeting and marrying my dad. I took after her and often resorted to drawing to ignore the fighting in the house caused by my father's drinking. My mom taught me how to sew clothes and knit. I recall my first pair of striped bell-bottom pants and my pride in putting in the zipper, and the first baby blanket I made for a doll.

My sister was five and a half years older than me. I don't honestly recall her being around much. She went to prep school in western New Jersey, and we would visit her occasionally on Sundays for lunch. But we didn't share a close bond since we had quite a bit of an age difference. My brother and I were very close, though. He was two and a half years younger than me. I remember he used to have issues with bronchitis, pneumonia, and other sicknesses. My mom cared for him when he got sick, but my dad accused her of babying him. I was my father's favorite since I was the most low-maintenance child.

He took me skiing with him in Pennsylvania and New York State and taught me how to use the lift. I remember my dad whistling happily on these trips, excited to show me the next turnabout on the more difficult trails. I never saw him so relaxed and content at home.

Although I do recall a couple times when he hit me for some tiny mistake like using too many band-aids or spilling water while doing the dinner dishes. I was shocked but almost expected it. I knew there was always an underlying tension brewing below the surface. If I cried, he would say, "stop crying, or I'll give you something to cry about." One particular Christmas, my dad went ballistic about how much money my mom spent as we opened gifts. After such episodes, I learned to disassociate. I would go into my bedroom to listen to music and forget my parents' existence. I thought my dad would be happier and not need to drink and yell so much if we didn't spend money. If my mom bought me a nice outfit, I would say, "take it back. I don't want it." I assumed this was a big part of their arguments and thus saving money would endear all of us to him.

Chapter 2: Loss

Growing up in the 60s was a time of hippies, rock music, and a lot of drugs. I wore bell bottoms, fishnet stockings, and miniskirts. My friends and I spent Saturday nights drinking at Steak & Brew, followed by oldies concerts at Madison Square Garden, dancing to Chuck Berry and Fats Domino. I don't recall my parents ever wondering where we were or whether we were safe taking the last subway out of NYC after a night of partying.

During my sophomore year in high school, my parents bought a house on Lake Naomi in Pennsylvania. I migrated toward the "townies" and learned to appreciate the J. Giles Band and country rock 'n' roll at night, smoking cigarettes and getting high by the lake.

I kept busy sailing in the nice weather, skiing during winter, and waitressing at the Motor Lodge. My mom started an affair with the contractor, hired to build additions to our house. When I questioned her, my mom justified it based on my father's "annoying habit" of getting drunk in the middle of the day. I developed a certain level of bitterness towards both of my parents because of how they behaved. It felt so back-stabbing and careless to me. If they didn't care about their lives or each other, what was I doing besides pretending?

By 1973, I couldn't wait to leave for college in Massachusetts. The campus was considered a "suitcase college" since it attracted a lot of locals, and everyone went home on the weekends. Often, they would take me home with them. I felt slightly removed from myself, sitting at their dinner tables with parents who seemed comfortable with each other, joking and having fun together. It felt so alien to me; I almost became homesick for a different version of my life that never existed. By Thanksgiving, I was looking forward to seeing my family again. I'd never been away so long and almost missed them. I recall a friend saying, "I hope it's all that you think it's going to be."

For a while, everything in my life went on steadily. My friends at college drank a lot. I drank too, but I didn't let drinking consume me. I didn't want to be the same way my dad was. I wanted to be different from him. I started to relax and appreciate the moments of freedom I got to experience. Still, the bubble of stability would soon burst during the extra-long Christmas break of my first year.

Growing up, I always enjoyed going to my grandparent's house for the holidays because my parents didn't fight in front of them. My grandmother would surprise us kids with ice cream or other treats. They took all the grandchildren to the circus at Madison Square Garden every year. They bought us chameleon lizards as we watched the acts. I felt safe with my grandparents because they never argued. My mom was extremely close with her folks. Since they lived within a few miles of our home, she saw them a few times a week.

When my mother couldn't reach her parents for a couple of days, she went to their house to find the mailbox overflowing and newspapers on the walk. She got a neighbor to call the police. On January 4, 1974, I vividly remembered my folks walking toward the house at midday, escorted by policemen. My father never missed a day of work or came home early, but he was there that day, so I knew something was terribly wrong. Both my grandparents had been found dead in their home.

We don't really know what happened. It was said that my grandmother suffered a heart attack while eating dinner in front of the TV, and my grandfather panicked and had a heart attack watching her. I recall hearing they were found slumped over on the couch together, TV blaring to no one. It seemed like such an innocent, normal day to suddenly die.

The funeral home was packed with friends and family that loved Marie and Bob. They were married many years and were considered love birds. The two coffins were touching each other at the front of the church, surrounded by hundreds of beautiful flower arrangements.

The devastation my mother was left with after losing both her beloved parents in one afternoon was overwhelming. She started wearing dark glasses everywhere since her eyes were always red from crying. There was nothing anyone could do to help her, least of all me.

My mother's financial situation changed overnight, and she left my father after twenty-five years of a very trying marriage. She always justified staying that long by saying, "I would never have had you three wonderful children if I hadn't been with your father." I later carried that philosophy into my own marriage. I came to believe that this was true.

Six months later, she was diagnosed with breast cancer.

Chapter 3: Dealing With Illness

After my parents legally separated, my mom stayed in the Poconos to receive radiation for her cancer, which we all believed would be treatable. She thrived without my father, spending days with boyfriend and her cocker spaniel. She loved the house and the area. Her front yard was a rock garden where blueberries grew wild. She gardened and baked and enjoyed the daylilies by the driveway.

My mom enjoyed music and dancing, so we would visit with a tape player and boogie to Bob Seiger and The Rolling Stones. She loved Elvis and Englebert Humperdinck and Tom Jones and cried when Elvis died.

My dad was back in New Jersey trying to date and stay sober but failed to. I spent alternating work breaks visiting them from Massachusetts, worried about his health and my mom's. One night my father woke me sobbing about how much he missed my mom. "I still love your mother. I'm so lonely without her. Please tell her I want her back." I was very confused since I thought he hated her. There was nothing I could say or do to make him stop crying. It was awful. I had never seen him cry before.

The next day I left for Massachusetts; weeks passed before I heard from him again. Eventually, we talked; I remember he had been trying to stay sober but couldn't. I encouraged him over and over again to no avail. I transferred to colleges in Massachusetts to live closer to my parents. I spent weekends watching my mother deteriorate and bounce back with every doctor's visit, mastectomy, reconstruction, and radiation. It was months of getting our hopes up, only to be struck down again. Cancer had a way of disrupting everything in its path, and I struggled to bear witness to the destruction that it caused. My father lived a completely separate life and never really knew the extent of my mother's cancer. None of us did.

My vagabond lifestyle kicked in. Although I had moved close by and went home from college every weekend to help her. I managed to take care of her while she was sick and struggled to find motivation for school amidst everything going on. For a period of time, my mom seemed to be recovering well and was happily in love with her boyfriend. Four friends from college had moved out west and invited me to join them in Colorado, and with my mom's blessing, I dropped out of college and ran. Everything wasn't fine, but it seemed that way temporarily.

My first impression of the Rocky Mountains was endless snow and pine trees. It was January, and we four college girls lived in a timber log cabin heated with a single wood-burning stove. There was no electricity or running water. We could see through holes in the broken walls to the freezing winter outside, but we didn't care. We spent our days collecting kindling for the fire, hiking into the foothills, and venturing into town for groceries and showers. It was a much-needed escape from my life at home.

I was only supposed to stay for two weeks but kept calling my mom up to ask for more clothes as the seasons changed. By the time I finally went home, it was late June. My mother's cancer treatments had been deemed successful. As I walked toward her from the driveway, even after the passage of so much time, I felt her beautiful spirit and unconditional love for me. We lived near the Pocono racetrack and went to a couple of car races that summer. There was a lot of drinking and partying in the stands, and I observed how wild people became when getting drunk. I struggled with not comparing others to my dad when they were puking off the side of the track. I felt sorry for him and missed him.

I didn't want to stay in the Poconos, so I moved back to Massachusetts and lived close to the ocean in Newburyport. I was a waitress at the Grog restaurant, where I met and fell in love with the bartender. At first, we were very compatible, but soon enough, the cracks in the relationship revealed themselves. His mom was institutionalized for paranoid schizophrenia when he was two years old.

He began accusing me of having an affair when I went to the grocery store. I became afraid of his violent outbursts. I was used to alcoholic behavior, but this was on an entirely different level.

My mom had a brother she was very close with before and during losing their parents. He took over the lithography business my grandfather had started in NYC and figured out all the logistics between the funeral, the selling of the house, and the finances. My mom was dependent on him for moral support also. Uncle Bud, Aunt Barbara, and my three cousins lived next door to us in NJ, and we spent lots of time with them. He taught me how to ride a bike and throw a softball when I was trying to accomplish the presidential award in high school.

In October 1977, I went to visit my mom in Pennsylvania for the weekend. I walked in the front door, and she was again in her fuzzy blue robe. She looked like "death warmed over."

I asked, "What happened? What's wrong?"

She sobbed in my arms. "Uncle Bud died. He was playing paddle tennis yesterday and died of a heart attack."

Her frail body sunk into mine. I was devastated. She was too weak to handle another loss. His funeral was held in NJ the following week, and she couldn't gather the energy to go. I went, and hundreds of people were there, just like at my grandparent's funeral.

I continued visiting between my parents, trying to placate the divorce decisions and help out as much as possible. I was barely 24 years old and scared and worried about my father living much longer, let alone my mom.

In April 1979, a neighbor noticed my father hadn't been around for a few days and called the police to check on the house. He was found dead in his bed of a heart attack. When we told my mom, she was absolutely devastated. I drove home, and when I walked into the house, I was shocked. My mom has dressed in her fuzzy blue bathrobe again and could barely speak. She had aged dramatically between her health and these profound losses in a few weeks. I think she hoped we three kids would have one parent around since she probably knew her cancer was winning by that time. I still didn't realize. I attended my father's funeral and can't remember where my siblings were. It seemed we needed to care for my mom, but I looked around and felt completely alone. Loss after loss left my life in a blur.

Days of radiation, a mastectomy, doctors, chemotherapy, and blood transfusions defined the next few weeks. Three months before she died, I was standing in front of an X-ray machine as the curt doctor quickly put up a slide of yet another grapefruit-size tumor and said, "there is nothing else we can do."

I stared at him in disbelief. First, it was breast cancer. Then it began spreading to the bone, lungs, and the brain as well. My mom was sent home, and I stayed with her, but I didn't know what to do. I thought surely someone would show up and help me. I drove her back and forth to Geisinger Medical Center daily for her treatments.

She lost her hair; I bought her wigs. She lost her appetite; I cried when she wouldn't eat dinner. I took care of her, and a tiny part of me believed that if I did the right things, she would live forever. She asked for "good cookies, not those fig newtons." I was always trying to feed her well so she would get better. When she wrote on the grocery list, her handwriting was a scribble. Her peripheral vision was off from the tumor pushing on her brain.

One day, she cried, "I only wish I could see your sister have a baby and you get married." This was the only time I heard any defeat in her voice.

On a warm, sunny day on July 15th, 1979, my mom woke from her nap and couldn't breathe. I quickly called an ambulance and packed a bag for the night. I rode in the ambulance, holding her frail hand.

"Don't worry, you'll be back home again tomorrow," I promised.

By dawn, she had been struggling all night; her lungs were filling up with fluid. Seeing her pleading eyes with the oxygen mask hiding her beautiful smile was awful. She was panting as her breathing became more and more labored as the hours ticked by.

We took turns saying "I love you" while the nurses came in to make her more comfortable. Nothing helped.

The chaplain prayed for us. A few weeks ago, my sister, brother-in-law, and I decided we wouldn't put her on a ventilator. So this was it - things were not going to get any better. Even then, I still didn't quite realize she was going to die.

My mind now ricochets to holding my mother's hand when she took her last breath. I was unprepared to survive without her. I remember the hospital room, the clouds, the feeling of being released, of her leaving me stranded on earth. I was only twenty-four years old and felt my insides tremble with weakness. My pain was so great I felt like I was spilling out from an open wound from my pubic bone to the top of my chest, and every day, in tiny increments, the scar would close up a fraction. One day I was whole again on the outside, but my heart and soul still ached forever for the loss. When I lost my mom, everything from that moment on was defined as "before she died" and "after my mother was gone."

As a caretaker, I didn't create a life for myself outside of being with my mother. I didn't have any friends or a career to fall back on. I worked for a young dentist who opened a new practice nearby. I was sensitive to his curt demands and cried on my lunch breaks. "I'm so sorry I spoke to you like that," he'd apologize. It really had nothing to do with him. I was just sad and lonely every day. No matter what I did or didn't do, I never felt good enough; I felt so depressed.

I begged God to let me just see her one more time for a while, and then I could go on without her. I took the sailboat out on the lake on a very windy winter day and had huge problems returning to shore. I was scared, but deep down, I thought I wanted to die and be with my mom again.

Chapter 4: Wishful Thinking

The following summer, my sister, her husband, and I bought a house together at the Jersey Shore. We sold my mom's house in the Poconos and migrated back to the big, blue ocean.

Just as I was getting my life in order, the arrows of Cupid struck and completely rattled me. In a few years, I fell in love with Mike, Mark, and Jeff. During that time, I felt like the puppy in the pound window:

"Pick me, pick me." My heart kept whispering incessantly.

I wanted to be loved, appreciated, and happy. Although Cupid's arrows had struck me thrice, I chose to marry Jeff, my so-called soul mate. But I didn't understand the deep pattern I inherited from my father's alcoholism. It created a lifetime of falling for men who drank excessively and me subconsciously trying to fix them.

Chapter 5: Hope

In August 2007, my husband lost all hope and committed suicide. Jeff struggled with alcoholism, depression, and inner demons throughout our marriage. I had also lost all hope for our life together and filed for divorce the year before. Our lives were a constant struggle; me against him, and he against his powerful and insidious addiction. I wince and turn away when I think of what he did in desperation.

This is the story of my husband's tragic path toward self-destruction and my subsequent recovery from years of emotional abuse and personal despair. In the end, it destroyed Jeff and nearly destroyed me.

When I fell in love with Jeff, I thought it would be forever. I never knew it could be so difficult for so long. The beginning together is hard to recall, and the ending is impossible to forget. Jeff's addiction stole his life very slowly and subtly until it was bigger than everything else. Addiction is a terminal disease, but people don't have to die from it; this is the story of one man who did. Jeff's life became a constant struggle to survive; in the end, suicide was his victory.

Some people just can't be saved. Jeff tumbled into a dark pit of despair. There was no turning back as he suffered so. I was overcome with anger, confusion, and sadness for much of our life together. My heart hurt, and I cried for our innocent children affected by this disease. I believed our life together would be so complete and happy that he wouldn't need liquor. Eventually, we didn't have the resiliency to face this challenge and stay strong as a couple. He turned out to be one of those alcoholics who didn't have the capacity for the honesty needed to get better. Alcoholism defeated us, and we lost our equilibrium. Although I despised what he did, I feel I must defend his decision. I also forgive him. I simply would pay too high a price if I refused. True forgiveness is letting go of all our ledgers of injustice and retribution and, with open arms remembering only the heart and goodness of a person we loved.

The poet Anne Sexton wrote, "It's not who your father really was, it's who you remember him to be." Both our children had a natural tolerance and compassion for their dad. I know Jeff's love for them will remain in their hearts forever. I want them to remember the smart, funny, and talented father who loved them dearly and unconditionally. Not the dad who was so desperately ill that he chose death instead of life. Kevin and Kelsey were the light of his life, his greatest accomplishment, his only pure joy in the darkness of his spiraling addiction.

My story is different but by no means unique. The devastation of alcohol addiction and suicide is played out within families worldwide. I hope to reach out to those who have been through similar losses, educate people about the ravages of this disease, and hopefully provide some measure of support for those affected by both alcoholism and suicide. If my words can help even one suffering person, I will know that my efforts were not in vain.

Toward the end of Jeff's life, I knew there was nothing more I could do to help him. He would have dragged me into his darkness before I could have led him into the light. The difference between us is that I never gave up hope for a better life for myself and my children.

My message is to continue to hope, no matter how difficult your days may be. Life is not always perfect; neither is it predictable, but giving up hope means giving in to this disease. To me, being a victim was no longer an option.

Chapter 6: The Final Curtain

I knew it was over in the thick heat of another summer's night. Jeff had been missing already since the day before. Quietly and systematically, he was on a path of self-destruction.

The cicadas were singing, and life on the street was going on around me, but I was filled with forebodings of disaster. When I saw the ominous sight of the police car pull up and turn around in the neighbor's driveway and then stop between the houses, I went outside and sat on the front step.

I waited for hours; I could see they were on the phone and never came to the door, so I went back inside. When they spoke to a neighbor a while later about who lived here, I thought they would come and speak to me soon.

I was just waiting in limbo. There was a breathless silence as I emerged from the house a second time for a moment. I had a premonition because of the previous suicide attempt. When the police finally came to the door, I knew what they needed to say.

The doorbell rang, and I knew immediately that my husband was dead.

"Are you Mrs. Lund?" the heavy-set detective asked.

Jeff had been missing for two days since checking out of the rehab center at Saint Clare's Hospital. He had attempted suicide three weeks before.

"Y...y...ess," I whispered. I slowly stepped out onto the front steps. Cicadas were singing, and the mid-August air was thick and still. The sky was aglow with warm pink tones, signaling the end of another hot, humid summer day.

"Mrs. Lund, I have some terrible news for you."

"Please," I begged the officers, "just tell me what he did."

The policeman sighed and planted his feet. "He committed suicide, ma'am. We found him earlier today."

My knees buckled. *Oh God, how could he do this?* I covered my face and let out a primal scream.

The officer reached down to touch my shoulder. "Is there anyone we can call to be with you?"

"My son," I sobbed. Their arms carried me through the door and into the front hallway of my house.

Kevin, my twenty-one-year-old son, was home from college. He was upstairs on his computer. When I appeared in his doorway, his face twisted in confusion. I paused, barely able to comprehend the words, no less speak them.

"Dad's dead," I cried.

"Nooooo!" Kevin cried as he blindly reached for my waiting arms. My heart sank as I realized his world, *our* world, would never be the same.

Kevin was no stranger to his father's violent and unpredictable behavior. Until the last few months of Jeff's life, when he was on the run, and his disease had taken over, Kevin had shared a close relationship with his dad. Jeff used to call him "Champ."

As Kevin grew up, Jeff had taken such pride in his accomplishments—watching him score the winning goal in a soccer game as a little boy and surf the Jersey Shore waves as a young man. Standing in Kevin's room surrounded by photos of the two of them in happier moments, it felt surreal to know that Jeff would never be coming home. I knew in my heart that Kevin didn't deserve to hear that his dad had killed himself in a lonely, strange hotel room and bled to death.

I felt crippling pain as I realized what this meant for him. Later, the detective waiting in my living room told me that a chambermaid had found Jeff in a hotel room in Parsippany, New Jersey. I assumed Jeff had re-slit his damaged wrists from his brutal suicide attempt the previous month but would not know all of the details of how he died until a few weeks later.

After the police left, I sat outside and called my closest friends and family. They knew what our family had been dealing with lately, but we were still shocked when I told them the news. They held me up with their hugs and kind words. Most of the conversations weren't even about Jeff or his death. I could force out a few smiles, but I was numb, and they knew it. How could I ever repay these women for being there at my darkest moment?

Meanwhile, my thirteen-year-old daughter, Kelsey, came home from next door. I dreaded having to say the words again. But I needed to get them over with. As she came up the front walk, I met her. I said simply, "Daddy's dead."

Stunned, she cried out, "But that's impossible; I just got a message on my cell phone from him saying he wanted to get together and take me out to lunch and shopping! He wouldn't have said those things if he didn't want to see me!" I had to put aside my grief when I realized my little girl's world was crashing down around her.

I cradled her in my arms as she sobbed out loud. "I know he wanted to be with you," I said, "but your father was sick. He loved you very much." What more could I say? I could barely comprehend the news myself. How could I expect her to? Later, after everyone had left, I tried to escape to the safety and comfort of my bed. I dozed on and off all night. I would open my eyes and know something was terribly wrong. *Oh right,* I thought, *something is terribly wrong! Jeff just committed suicide!* Now I needed to figure out how to continue living with this reality for the rest of my life.

Where do we go from here? The hope, faith, and prayers that carried us through those dark days led me to believe that the legacy could be better than alcohol and suicide: our children's legacy could be positive, powerful, and enlightening to others. I incorporated the many good qualities Jeff had into my relationship with them. He had a wonderful, dry sense of humor and wit that made people almost applaud him. Jeff was loyal and courageous. I admired his strength when he tried to address his unhappy childhood with a therapist. His sister, Sue, absolutely adored him, as did his two children. He had qualities that everyone gravitated to naturally until his addiction took over and he became an active alcoholic.

Jeff's greatest joy was in his son and daughter, and he tried to be the best dad in the world. He adored them and always wanted the best for them. He may not have loved himself, but he loved them more than life.

When I fell in love with Jeff, I thought it would be forever. I didn't know it would be so difficult for so many years. The beginning is hard to remember, and the ending is hard to forget. I'm not sure I need to do either to continue my life. Today, I accept what is and what is no longer. I want to find a balance between remembering Jeff and feeling a measure of comfort without him. Honestly, I can only give my children new beginnings and hope for the future.

Chapter 7: The Healing

The nightmare of Jeff's addiction, DUIs, and legal and financial problems was over for him, but they were just beginning for me. As I began to shuffle through the mountains of medical forms, past-due bills, collection agency notices, and junk mail, the loss and ache of twenty-three years of his addiction began to consume me. One minute, I felt guilty and sad. The next, I was angry. I had a hard time absorbing all that had happened. Jeff's life may have been a series of failures, but I never thought it would end like this.

That sweltering summer night, my husband, the love of my life, died from the love of his life: alcohol. I asked myself repeatedly, "What could I have done differently?" After the excruciating horror of Jeff's suicide was over, the great weight of the days began. I was so distraught that, at times, I would have to pull over to the side of the road because I was crying so hard that I couldn't see. Other days, I couldn't let myself cry because I thought if I started, I would never stop. During countless grief-stricken nights, I sat up until dawn, fearing that my own sanity was slipping away. I moved through my days in numb, slow motion, trying to keep some semblance of order at home for my children's adjustment to life without their father.

That fall, I spent my days obsessing over how Jeff could take his own life. Guiltily, I thought, why wasn't I able to stop him? Maybe if I had picked him up from the rehabilitation center that morning and helped him get settled in his apartment, I could have saved him. Maybe if I had been more tolerant of his alcoholism and remained in the marriage, he wouldn't have resorted to taking his life. I was tormented by the "maybes." Yet, over time, I realized that Jeff had been determined to take his life no matter what I had ever said or done to help him. There was nothing I could have done to change the outcome.

I thought back over the final months of Jeff's life, and again, feelings of guilt came back to haunt me. His first suicide attempt, his worsening alcoholism, his mounting debt, shrinking bank accounts, and major depression were huge red flags. Yet none of us knew just how fragile he was. He had been on the run for weeks; he had slipped away without anyone knowing what was happening. Sadly, I regret not trying harder to locate him or to understand just how pathetic a state he was in.

To answer my nagging questions about his suicide, I read any books I could on depression, bipolar disorder, alcoholism, and suicide. I talked to a grief counselor, joined a suicide survivors' group, and continued to educate myself on alcohol addiction. I discovered that suicide is not carried out exclusively by insane or mentally ill people, although who else would do this? I also learned that alcoholism does not discriminate. It affects people in all walks of life, from high-powered executives to skid row bums. As I began to process these hard, cold facts, the puzzle pieces began to fit together. Things began to make sense, and my agony began to subside. I now know many factors influence a person's decision to commit suicide. The actual act is a release because it appears as a way to have balance and order in a dysfunctional life. People who commit suicide are trying to control their out-of-control lives. Death is just an act to end their unendurable pain. Jeff's mental anguish was so intense that it outweighed the physical pain of dying.

I could have spent my energy trying to understand Jeff's troubled soul to find more answers, but in the months after his death, I began to accept his suicide. I forgave him for what he had done. This forgiveness freed me to move beyond my own pain. Today, I know he was an unwilling victim of the disease of alcoholism. It was never his choice to continue on such a destructive path. I now have compassion and empathy for all he endured.

By Thanksgiving of that year, I came to believe that the anguish of Jeff's addiction and the toll of his death would lift. My legal and financial issues were still unresolved, but I felt like I was beginning to rise back to the surface. I didn't cry nearly as much. I slept much better. I could go for long stretches without thinking about the horror of what I had just been through. I could even smile about some of the happy times we had as a family.

I had lunch with a friend who listened compassionately for years about my difficult partner. She heard me justify and defend staying in the marriage and plead to get out in the same sentence. I hear other voices of women who are confused between love and control. It's very slow and subtle, almost unnoticeable daily or even yearly. Until one day, you realize something is wrong and that this is not what you want. Beyond a reasonable doubt, our lives had centered around Jeff's alcoholic behavior for the entire marriage. We were kept off-balance, even when things seemed steady and reliable. Jeff could go from "zero to ten" in two seconds flat.

I would grasp at straws to comprehend why Jeff screamed at Kevin over ketchup packets or at me because I said, "It's OK, skip the ketchup on the burger." What purpose would even be winning that argument has served: to establish who was more insane? (Him or me?) Hands down—I am! Because I was stone-cold sober and still crazy enough to engage and try to reason with him. I wasn't trying to be rebellious or even hostile, but I did feel the need to defend. As Kevin got older, I left them to their own battles.

For the first time in over two decades, I was no longer controlled by Jeff's disease. I could focus on my own life and set a new path for my future. I can't believe I don't interact with anyone like that anymore. It's surreal to remain at peace throughout the day. No one is "furious" with me because I didn't pick up the milk. With every shred of reason, I wanted to understand and placate, pretend and minimize so that the insanity didn't matter. I continuously balanced on a tightrope while keeping many balls in the air.

I think back to happier times, but I'm not nostalgic in a sad way. I was proud when Kevin was born, and Jeff whisked him off to change his diaper and play with him. I recall the laughter and hugs that we shared. I have many fond memories, and I don't want to forget them. I made plenty of mistakes, blamed myself for his sickness, and struggled with guilt, but I have survived.

The journey details are becoming a bit blurry as the years go by. Searching for a balance, I can feel a feeling of peace with Jeff's suicide. It's been an effort to stay afloat, not drown in self-doubt, self-pity, and sorrow. I feel fortunate to have survived so much turmoil and despair with love and faith. There is a thin line between remembering, focusing on, and living in that frame of mind enough to be able to put down on paper what I want to and moving beyond the pain.

My mind wants to escape the trauma and forget, but I need to dwell a little longer in the trenches to tell my story. Was Jeff destined to die this way even before he was born? Is even my greatest joy on any given day going to be tinged with a sense of sadness because of his death?

Chapter 8: History Repeats Itself

I met Jeff when I was twenty-eight years of age in the spring of 1982 through a mutual friend who was one of his many roommates for the upcoming summer in Belmar, New Jersey. Craig had had a hunch about the two of us and insisted that we meet after one of their weekly baseball games. I remember Jeff running off the field to meet me.

He was tall and slim but solidly built. His sweaty, auburn hair was tousled and matted against his forehead. His soft, brown eyes spoke to me, and I was instantly attracted. We planned to sail the next day, and I joked about how bad a sailor I was. Jeff just smiled and laughed along with me. He and Craig lobbed jokes back and forth about the game and their antics on the field. Jeff could take a joke as well as make one. I could tell he was a fun guy to be around.

That night, we all went out for pizza at a local hangout. Jeff and I sat next to each other at the tiny table. The subject of birthdays came up. We discovered that we were born on the same day, two years apart. I felt like meeting this guy was fate. From that night on, I knew Jeff would be a part of my life. How much or how long would remain to be seen.

On our first date, I told Jeff about my mother dying of breast cancer three years before. Then he told me about losing his mom to lung cancer the same year. Suddenly, we had another deep, visceral connection. After several dates, we fell in love. I knew I didn't want to date anyone else but Jeff.

Jeff told me about his family. His dad and sister lived close by, and he would stop in frequently to visit. From what I could gather, they were a close-knit family, especially after his mom had passed away. When I finally met them, I liked them instantly. I felt close to them, just as I did with my own family. When I brought Jeff to meet my family, they liked him too.

Jeff was a true gentleman. He would always pick me up on time, hold the door for me, or pull out my chair to be seated. He was considerate about letting me decide what we should do or where we should go. We spent our time going on dates or hanging out with our extended friends at local bars. Jeff would have a few beers but never overindulge. He was disciplined and always in control. He even convinced me to quit smoking, and I finally did because I loved him so much. I didn't want him to disapprove of anything I did.

Jeff was the first man I had dated who didn't appear to be a heavy drinker. My father was an alcoholic, and not surprisingly, I had always gravitated toward men like him. Jeff was so different. He was soft-spoken and calm. He didn't need alcohol to loosen up; he was settled, responsible, and comfortable with himself. He was also fun without being crazy, a new concept for me. My previous boyfriends were all "life-of-the-party" type guys. It felt good to be with a man who loved life and didn't drink heavily. I couldn't believe that I was with a man who was so *normal.*

I never found drinking much fun, but I was drawn to "exciting" men who were full of fun and drinkers living on the edge. They were always a little wild, and that appealed to me. Most were undoubtedly alcoholics. Others were just college kids experimenting. My relationships with these men were chaotic and unpredictable.

They called the shots, and I followed and watched. I found ways to survive the tremendous impact alcoholism had on my life and self-image. I could have made more damaging choices. It is said that many girls "marry their fathers," and I did. My childhood was being replayed with Jeff. All the clues of alcoholic predisposition were there, but I simply failed to see them. I loved him fiercely.

Jeff always encouraged me to go out with my friends or visit my family. He was never jealous or possessive and wanted me to continue to be the independent woman that I was. I, on the other hand, felt protective of Jeff. He was shy and quiet, and I felt he needed my motherly affection. I wanted to take care of him so he would love me in return. That fall,

Jeff moved to a house in Parsippany with a few guys. I lived in Chatham in a home I bought after my parents died. We spent more time together, riding bikes, hiking, playing racquetball, and going to movies and dinner together. We would sit and banter back and forth and find a similar sense of humor. I laughed when he told me stories about his roommates' antics or the people he worked with.

I was ready for him to propose. I had met my Prince Charming and would live happily ever after. We experienced the dopamine high as the year-long relationship grew. Jeff was romantic and fun. I felt we truly connected with each other and were good together. A few weeks later, he asked me to marry him, and I felt confident about our decision.

I excitedly accepted the engagement ring and enjoyed blissful weeks of telling friends and family. Everyone loved Jeff and me together. We experienced a rejuvenated, young, and giddy love. I felt like a huge weight had been lifted since I was with my "soul mate," and we could plan for the future. I had a new determination that I would go a new way: different from my childhood.

On that beautiful day in the spring of 1983, Jeff proposed to me at my summer home in Lavallette, at the Jersey Shore. With his boyish grin, he kneeled before me and asked me to marry him. I was so excited that I got my answer before he could finish.

He handed me a small box. Inside was the diamond from my mother's engagement ring that he had had reset. It was just what I had dreamed of. Afterward, we dined on lobster at Krone's restaurant and shared a bottle of wine in celebration. Summer was just around the corner, and life couldn't have been sweeter. We were two kids happily in love, with the promise of married life ahead of us.

We got right to work planning the wedding. It was entirely up to us without my parents or Jeff's mom. I had always dreamed of making my own wedding dress and bridesmaids' gowns, so every night after work, I got behind my sewing machine, busily creating them. Jeff never complained about our time apart. He understood that I couldn't be with him all the time. When we were together, we spent long hours talking about our plans, hopes, and dreams for the future. We always agreed on everything. We were like true soul mates.

When we married on April 7, 1984, at Saint Paul's Church in Chatham, New Jersey, I was the happiest girl on earth. We scheduled the ceremony at 11:00 a.m. and the reception at noon because neither of us was night owls. Our wedding was formal but simple. I walked down the aisle with my brother at my side and saw Jeff waiting for me at the altar. He was beaming. We looked into each other's eyes and knew at once that we were meant to be together. We danced the day away and dined on fabulous food in the sun-filled atrium at the lovely Madison Hotel.

We honeymooned at a resort in Barbados and snorkeled, ate extravagant dinners, watched glorious Caribbean sunsets, and relaxed on the beach. At lunch, we would have a cocktail or two, and then over dinner, we would share a bottle of wine. One day, we took a cruise on the good ship *Jolly Roger*. Jeff drank a few too many rum punches and was rip-roaring drunk along with everyone else on the boat.

I was shocked. I had never seen him drunk before. I must have been the only sober soul on the cruise. That evening, he was quiet and sorry that he had gotten so drunk. I forgave him instantly. After all, it was our honeymoon, and I didn't want to ruin it by getting mad at him for such a minor indiscretion.

After a week in paradise, we returned to the routines of our lives. I went back to work as a receptionist for a doctor in town, and Jeff went back to his job in human resources at a local company. We phoned each other every day to say, "See you at five-thirty; I love you." After work, I would shop for groceries and pick up a few six-packs of beer for Jeff. Initially, he would come home and pay the bills or putter around the workbench in the garage. Over the coming weeks, though, Jeff began to sit in the backyard and drink beer while I made dinner. I wasn't concerned at first.

After all, everyone I knew had a cocktail or two to unwind after a stressful day at work.

We were lucky enough to start our married lives without financial struggles. Because I owned a furnished home in a nice town, we had instant stability. I also owned half of a second home at the Jersey Shore and had a comfortable nest egg in the bank. Jeff liked that I was financially independent and that I didn't keep any secrets from him about who I was or what I owned.

Since I had bought the homes, he wanted to contribute to their month-to-month maintenance. He took over paying the bills out of his paycheck and handled all the upkeep on the homes. I appreciated his effort to lighten my financial load and homeowner responsibilities, and he seemed to enjoy mowing the lawn and fixing up our homes. Our lives were falling into place, and I could not have been happier.

Drinking became an issue within the first couple of weeks of our marriage when the cases of beer I bought twice a week disappeared within days. Jeff was easily consuming a six-pack every night to unwind after work. I was beginning to worry. "Why are you drinking every night?" I would ask. He would turn and sneer at me. I had never seen him look at me like that before. "I'm not doing anything wrong; leave me alone!" he would shout.

I was the perfect enabler by buying the beer and then complaining to him that he was drinking too much. He screamed at me, "I'm not your father!" The color drained from my face. No one had ever yelled at me like this before. I became smaller and smaller every time he raged at me. I was a very independent woman when we met, but I slowly gave up more of myself to try and make him happy. His drinking became more prevalent no matter what I did or didn't do.

My father didn't bother me at all compared to my husband with his drinking. Still, I was programmed to choose this character in a man to try and fix my relationship with my dad. The battle lines were being drawn. I felt conned, lied to. This was not the person I knew before we were married. But I couldn't just leave like the other relationships. I felt stuck.

Everything in our marriage had been so perfect. Why was he suddenly drinking and yelling at me like this? I wanted desperately to make Jeff happy, so I continued to buy the beer and watch him drink in silence. I even pretended it didn't bother me. Sometimes I would join him outside but never drink along with him. How could I drink with him when I was complaining about him doing it? Besides, I didn't need beer to help me relax. I exercised to unwind. I wanted to keep doing the fun things that we had done together before we were married and secretly resented him sitting and wasting away drinking beer in the backyard. I thought back to my own childhood and how painful and dysfunctional it had been. My father had been a raging alcoholic and verbally abusive to my mother and siblings. We always tiptoed around "the elephant in the living room" and pretended nothing was wrong. From a young age, I remember trying to please him and my mother by overcompensating and taking on too much responsibility. I also didn't want to make waves and tried to keep a low profile around them. I thought that if I drew attention to myself, they would argue, and my father would have more reason to drink.

The smallest things would set him off. I remember how he sometimes went off on a tirade if he thought my mother had used too much water to wash the dishes. "Do you know how much this is costing me?" he would shout. Then she would scream back. Soon, doors were slamming, and they were in a heated argument—usually over something equally ridiculous. My brother and I pretended not to notice the yelling in the other room, but the effect was profound. We witnessed what was happening, and it changed us on a cellular level. We never cared who was wrong or right. We simply wanted the intense screaming matches to stop. As my parents argued every moment, they were together, I shut down and ignored them, except for a few sparse memories.

My dad called my mom a "kraut" since she was of German descent. I recall going to Washington, DC when my father couldn't find the hotel room's bathroom in his drunken stupor, so he threw up and peed in the closet. Another time, we were skiing, and he slammed the car door on my mother's finger and wasn't the least bit sorry or sympathetic. He just wanted to get to the bar to get a drink (which he called "hooch"). I recall my mom crying more about his disregard for her than her physical pain. But he was never kind or loving toward her. I don't know why she expected him to be any different.

We traveled as a family, which was torture for me since there was no way to escape the dissension between my parents. My father would freak out at the restaurants if we ordered food we didn't eat. We weren't at McDonald's with their dollar menu, and he became crazy when the bill came. I just wanted to crawl under the tablecloth and pretend I wasn't alive. I truly hated to go on these three-week vacations with my family. Luckily, they happened only every few years.

When my father drank, we pretended not to notice. Later, when he sobered up, we pretended he was well but treated him with kid gloves since that was when we actually viewed him as sick. We were very mixed up. White lies were wishful thinking given a voice. Perhaps we believed that if we insisted, we were "one big, happy family," we would become one. The fun didn't come naturally to me when I was a little girl. I had already lost my God-given gift for play. My father was a solemn man; he sat stone-faced in his chair in the back room, smoked a pipe, and never cracked a smile. He belittled, insulted, and dominated my mother. I was repelled; I felt not even a trace of compassion—and I was his "favorite" of the three children. Substance-abuse issues dogged him for years, and he fell off the wagon repeatedly. Once we learned that alcoholism was a disease, we treated it as such—not as a moral failure.

The stress and friction in our house were so great that I dreaded being around. I didn't know what would set my father off. I walked on eggshells, always conscious of my actions and aware of every word uttered to keep him from mouthing off. He needed alcohol daily to blunt his inner desperation. A great weight lifted off my shoulders when I realized the truth. I had already been touched and deeply affected by alcoholism before I met and married Jeff, choosing unconsciously for myself a pattern of life familiar to me.

While growing up, my mother was hospitalized frequently for surgery. I was petrified that she wouldn't come home again and I would be left with my dad. With this anxiety and fear, I developed insomnia. While I couldn't sleep, I came downstairs to the den where mom was watching television. Sometimes, she sent me back to bed with a valium after I calmed down with her unconditional love. She was the safe haven in the storm of my childhood.

I believed I was being punished for something. I thought it was my job to fix or control what was wrong. I had many conversations with God and made promises that I would try to be perfect, bargaining that if my mother lived, I would never do anything wrong again. She died when I was twenty-four years old. I was filled with confusion and felt lost. What little family was left disintegrated. We each grieved privately and could not share our anguish with one another. At that point, I shut down emotionally. I learned that I feel hurt and never wanted to experience that kind of pain again.

We were a dysfunctional family, but we managed to keep up false pretenses for the outside world. Holidays were especially stressful. Each year, my mother would exhaust herself by shopping, cleaning, wrapping, and cooking to prepare for Christmas to give us kids a perfect day and a semblance of normality. My father did nothing but show up on Christmas morning, often hung over with a scowl. My dad went out to play paddle tennis on a particularly memorable one. Our gifts sat wrapped under the tree, but we were not allowed to open them until he came home. When he finally did, he began pounding gin and tonics. As we were opening our presents, he turned to my mother in a rage and said, "Why did you buy them so much stuff? It's all crap! I can't stand the way you spend money!" My mom was crushed. She burst into tears and ran out of the room. My siblings and I ran after her. By now, we were all crying too. Then, my father, in a rare moment of lucidity, tried to apologize to all of us. This was a pivotal moment for me. I realized just how sick and brutal a person my father could be.

Luckily, he would pass out on the couch after a couple of stiff drinks. He didn't argue anymore; he simply mumbled something unintelligible and slept. We carried on around him and pretended it wasn't unusual. It was better when he was asleep—instead of swearing, belittling, and shaming.

Our family lacked physical closeness and any semblance of communication, but I didn't equate any of that with alcoholism. I spent nineteen years living with this family disease and had no idea what I was dealing with. In fact, I thought it was normal. The most potent lessons I drew from my family situation were to stuff all my feelings deep into my subconscious and to become adept at the art of non-communication.

As a result of my dysfunctional upbringing, I had no frame of reference for healthy behavior. My coping skills were programmed, and I tended to automatically minimize or deny my true feelings. I had a "don't ask, don't tell" relationship with my father. I tried not to rock the boat. If I saw him out on the porch drinking, I would walk right by and avoid conversation. I knew not to ask about his drinking problem. I also knew not to tell anyone about what happened behind closed doors. There was no such thing as therapy in those days, either, so we kept our dysfunction a family secret. Over time, though, these secrets became my albatross. They became harder to shoulder and even harder to hide. I lost my sunny disposition. I became serious and constantly worried that people would find out about my dad, or worse, that my dad's drinking would be the undoing of my family.

My dad always left his large, half-gallon bottles of gin or bourbon right on the kitchen counter for all of us to see at the breakfast table the next morning. My mother would say, "Why doesn't your father put his liquor away?" How was I, a young child, supposed to know the answer to this question? Yet this became a normal part of my morning routine. I knew my dad had a problem. I wanted to do whatever I could to fix it. Despite his heavy drinking and tirades, my dad did have a soft side. He would take me horseback riding, bike riding, skiing, and occasionally to Palisades Amusement Park. He had boundless energy. He loved being outdoors and spending time with me when he was sober. Sadly, those fun weekends slowly gave way to weekends he spent holed up with a bottle of gin. I remember how I would find him stretched out on the couch any time of day or night, drunk or hung over. My father was a workaholic stockbroker who regularly entertained clients over lunch with a martini or two. He was brilliant and gregarious. Everybody loved Jack Cooke.

Amazingly, he never missed a day of work until the last year of his life, when his alcoholism had spun out of control. That year, my mother left him, and the company where he had worked for many years gave him an ultimatum: either check himself into the hospital or lose his job. He made several feeble attempts to become sober but was in and out of the hospital several times. He ultimately died alone in his bed of a heart attack when he was only fifty-nine years old.

My mother was a victim of a hopeless, loveless marriage. She was only able to separate from my father after she inherited money from her parents. Sadly, she developed breast cancer soon after she left my dad and struggled for five years with operations, radiation, and hospitalizations. She died just ten weeks after my dad. Losing her was the most devastating thing that has ever happened to me. Not surprisingly, I never felt this way about losing my dad. When I began dating, I knew that I did not want to date a man like my father. In fact, I was so traumatized by my parents' toxic marriage that, for a long time, I never wanted to marry. Yet somehow, every guy I dated ended up being an alcoholic. Was I subconsciously looking for a replacement for my father, even though I despised him and his alcoholism? Was I trying to punish myself for not fixing my father's alcoholism? It wasn't until I met Jeff that things changed. Suddenly, this new, sober, "nice" guy seemed like my knight in shining armor. He would be different from my dad. He would treat me like his princess and stay sober. He would be a good provider and a perfect father to my children.

When Jeff and I first met, it was love at first sight. Our meeting felt destined. He was charming, romantic, and sensitive. He projected a confident, carefree attitude that I found irresistible. He opened doors for me, guided me through a crowd with his hand on the small of my back, and made dinner reservations for us with other couples.

He showed me that he knew how to care for and appreciate me. We put each other on a pedestal, and I was blissfully happy. He called me his "Ivory girl" because I didn't wear makeup. I put up with his constantly changing moods because I loved him unconditionally. I had his undivided attention and affection. I was totally smitten. He had a dry sense of humor and cracked jokes that impressed me with his wittiness. He ramped up his comedy routine when I laughed at his humor. He was a go-with-the-flow, relatively quiet guy who was a good listener. He was empathetic and polite with a charmingly crooked grin. He was never scornful or superior; always just nice, kind, and gentle.

Our dating didn't revolve around drinking, but our relationship soon showed signs of wear and tear. I began to feel inadequate as a wife. We were newlyweds, but he insisted upon staying up to watch the late show and drink. He was a hard worker and loved me so much. I thought I could love him into sobriety. Within a few months after our marriage, though, Jeff began to rely more and more on beer to have fun, to relax, or just because he was bored. It was an all-too-familiar pattern that I was beginning to see.

When I asked him about it again, he screamed, "I'm not like your father; I don't drink that much!" Again, I was taken aback when Jeff reacted so vehemently. I knew he loved me. How could he be so mean and inconsiderate? I chalked it up to his inability to deal with the adjustment to married life.

Soon, however, Jeff began to exhibit other troubling tendencies, too. If I was on the phone, he would linger nearby and eavesdrop or interject with rude comments. I would ask him politely not to interrupt me. Then he would get angry or deny even doing anything.

He heard me say, "This is Sandy Cooke," during a phone call to a friend from high school. I told him I had used my maiden name because the person knew me before I had married and changed my last name.

Jeff wouldn't listen. He reprimanded me harshly. "You are married to me now, and you now use your married name, not your maiden name!" He was like Dr. Jekyll and Mr. Hyde. I was shocked that something as simple as this would set him off.

No one, not even my father, had ever yelled at me like that before. My father had graciously saved his tirades for my mother. I was completely caught off guard and was unprepared for how to deal with Jeff's transformation from a nice, reasonable husband to an insane control freak. I had many friends too, but soon Jeff became jealous of the time I spent with them. I found myself giving up a little bit more and more of my freedom as the months passed. Jeff's hold on me was powerful and seductive. I wanted to love this man with all my heart and to make him happy.

I began to doubt myself and lost my own identity with Jeff. For one hour, he could be sweet and lovable. The next, he could be belligerent and cold. This unpredictability kept me on my toes. After these angry outbursts, he would always apologize and be remorseful, and I always felt he was sincere. I learned how to tiptoe around him and guard my feelings to cope. I thought this was too reminiscent of my childhood, but Jeff wasn't my dad. I loved Jeff. I hated my dad.

As this pattern of on-again, off-again behavior continued, I felt I had relinquished part of my soul to my new husband. We were less than a year into our marriage, and I just couldn't understand what was wrong.

By our second anniversary, we got pregnant quite easily. We were both ecstatic. *Now,* I thought, *everything would be perfect.* Life will be good, and we will finally be happy. Jeff surprised me with a night at a fancy hotel. He was more romantic than me and tried hard to make amends for his not-so-perfect behavior. Eventually, though, Jeff began to come home from work to eat lunch. Behind my back, he would wash his turkey sandwich down with a beer or two and return to work. He started complaining more about his job and career, so I tried to think of ways to make him happier. Buying him beer was definitely one way I could do that. After all, I wanted to be the perfect wife!

He thought people were out to get him; they interfered with his plans they robbed him of the privileges, opportunities, and rewards to which he was entitled. It was much easier to excuse his behavior by pointing out failures in others than to admit his own shortcomings.

I started to notice more empty beer cans in the garbage. When I confronted Jeff about drinking during his lunch hour, he would shout at me and tell me he had drunk them the night before. I knew this wasn't true and continued to pry. He would snap back with, "Leave me alone; there is nothing wrong with a beer at lunch. I'm not like your father! I don't have a problem with booze!"

"I never said you were like my father! And yes, there is something wrong with drinking a beer at lunch by yourself!" I pointed out.

He'd get angrier and angrier, and I would become more and more submissive. Reasoning with him was out of the question. Nothing I said or would make any sense. The arguments usually ended with him twisting the truth around anyway. He made everything look like it was my fault and that I was a bad person for asking. Why didn't I just keep my big mouth shut? I remember calling my friend one night after an especially difficult argument. I sobbed into the phone as I described how distraught I was over my new husband's erratic behavior.

The unpredictable outbursts became more and more frequent. When I was eight months pregnant, we were driving to our friends' wedding. I wasn't able to read his scribbled directions. We made a wrong turn, and Jeff yelled, "Can't you just read what it says? Are you blind or something?"

"I can't read your writing," I said sheepishly.

He grabbed the paper out of my hands. "What's wrong with you? Can't you even follow simple directions?" he screamed.

I cried off and on during the wedding ceremony. How could I have been such a happy bride such a short time ago and now be so miserable? After the ceremony, Jeff apologized for his outburst and claimed that he wasn't feeling well when he yelled at me. He was sorry for being so impatient with me. I sat in silent bewilderment as I tried to comprehend the changes in my life. I never meant to provoke him—ever. I just wanted to please him. I just wanted us to be happy.

Chapter 9: A Baby

We welcomed our son, Kevin Eugene, into the world on September 24, 1985. Babies are huge milestones. I will never forget Jeff's look of utter joy when the doctor handed him his beautiful little bundle. He was a beaming—a proud dad in every sense of the word. Jeff was also a natural, which truly surprised me. He was gentle and knew just how to hold a baby. In the delivery room, he spoke soft words into Kevin's ear and caressed his soft, pink cheek. I had every reason to believe that Jeff would be a good dad.

Because I had had a C-section, I was in the hospital with Kevin for a week. Jeff came every day and brought me gifts and pampered me. More importantly, he was sober, which gave me hope that he might not need to drink. I felt like a queen—or a Princess Diana—for the first time in my life! Kevin was a perfect, beautiful baby. And we were the perfect little family. Jeff was euphoric about being a dad!

Even at home, we adjusted quickly to life with a baby. If Kevin was colicky, Jeff would sleep outside his crib and try to keep the pacifier in his mouth so I could get some much-needed sleep. During the evenings, Jeff would hold or bathe Kevin so I could have some time to myself. I thought having a baby was the best thing to happen to our marriage. Jeff had stopped coming home for a beer at lunch and seemed to be drinking less at night and on the weekends. We were getting along well, and things seemed to finally be falling into place.

I thought we had it all, with two houses, money in the bank, and a trying love between us. But lurking just below the surface in the not-so-far-off future were job losses, fertility issues, a major drinking problem, and hate for himself. Admitting my marriage was in a lot of trouble was scary for me. The elephant in the living room, bedroom, and kitchen sucked the air out of even our happiest moments.

A year later, we were moving into a bigger house hoping to expand our family. Jeff would come home every night and work on rebuilding the basement or steam wallpaper off the dining room walls. He took such pride in the work he did around the house. It was one of his many talents.

Jeff played sports on local teams with his buddies, partly to get some exercise and partly to channel some of his energy. He was a real guy's guy and loved a good, rough baseball, soccer, or pickup football game. After games, there were pitchers of beer and shots at the local bar. Sometimes the guys got together to play poker on Friday nights, too. Initially, I encouraged Jeff to go out and have fun. But then he started drinking so heavily that we would both pay for it the next day with Jeff's king-sized hangover. He would rationalize his nausea by saying he had food poisoning or a stomach virus. Who was he trying to fool?

When I rolled my eyes, invariably, he would say, "Why do you think I drank too much when I told you I didn't?" I'd tell him that I thought he had a drinking problem and was not happy about it. But he ignored me and continued to drink anyway.

There were mornings when Jeff was so hung over that his hands shook uncontrollably. Often, he would pop open another beer or two. It would help stop the shakes, he said. Then he'd go back to bed. Jeff's physical state became the barometer of how the day would go during this time. If he was well, I could relax. If he was ill, I cowered and stayed away. Even little Kevin knew when his dad wasn't feeling well. I knew it was best to keep Kevin out of the house at those times, so often, we would spend the day at the park or meet up with friends to see a movie.

Jeff's growing beer belly, swollen, red face, and sloppy, drunken behavior was obvious signs that he was drinking way too much. Now he didn't socialize or enjoy much of his life anymore. He turned into a recluse and chose to drink at home alone. This was just fine with Jeff. There was no one to judge how much he drank and no one to have to talk to. Plus, he didn't have to worry about driving home drunk. This withdrawal and growing isolation were yet another manifestation of Jeff's addiction to alcohol. It was beginning to dominate his life.

Life didn't resemble the "happily ever after" of fairy tales. We both grappled with our problems. He'd promise he'd stop drinking for good, and two days later, he'd be on another bender. I would ignore them when he had been drinking steadily for hours. Jeff felt guilty about his need to drink and found it easier to blame his drinking on me. He often provoked me, trying to start an argument or create a crisis. I tended to react to this, arguing back and defending myself against unjust accusations. Ultimately, Jeff got exactly what he was looking for: an excuse to drink. He used this tactic to create diversions to distract me from discussing an uncomfortable topic or situation. He continued to pit me against a disease I simply could not defeat. As long as I persisted in the delusion that I could control or cure Jeff of this disease, I continued fighting a battle I would never win.

I vowed to conquer this drinking business! I approached the problem with great zeal, counting bottles, emptying cans, and returning booze. I begged, scolded, nagged, and pleaded. My misplaced concern for him became intrusive, meddling, and resentful. This created discord in the marriage.

Meanwhile, Jeff's increasingly heavy drinking and surliness brought me to the most frightening realization. I had married someone similar to my father! Occasionally, we would still get together on a Sunday night with some friends who lived around the corner. Jeff thought this was a great way to keep the weekend party going.

We'd each bring a six-pack of beer, and after all of it was consumed, the host would offer more. Jeff had no problem putting away his six-pack and then some. (I, however, seldom drank for fear that I would become like my father.) One night, Jeff missed our street on the short drive home from our friend's house. It was the first time I saw him drive drunk. It brought a whole new layer of worry and concern to my already heavy anxiety. I could no longer trust him behind the wheel of a car.

Whatever Jeff had to drink was never enough. He could be slurring his words and stumbling, and yet he would reach for another beer. I would ask why he was having another and yell back, "Don't tell me how much beer I can have. If I want another one, I'll have another one. Leave me alone!" Then he would disappear into the basement, where he could peacefully drink all the beer he wanted. Without fail, he would be remorseful the next day. He would ask for forgiveness, sitting on the edge of the bed and holding his head.

"I'm so sorry; I don't know what got into me."

I would cry, knowing that this was just another false apology. "It's OK," I said, not wanting to make waves. "Don't worry about it." I could see that Jeff's problem was bigger than both of us. "Maybe you should talk to somebody about the problem," I added. But Jeff couldn't even accept that he had a problem. He would agree to try to get help, but it was just another lie.

We had certainly seen our fair share of troubles for a couple married just three years. Soon we had troubles of another kind, too: infertility. We had been trying for months to have another child. Each month that passed without a pregnancy made me feel guilty and stoked Jeff's feelings of inadequacy.

This became a huge sore point in our marriage and provided Jeff with another excuse to drink. We were arguing more, and, of course, I felt like a failure for not being able to make Jeff happy. During this time, he lost his job, probably because of erratic behavior related to his drinking. He was cynical and depressed. He followed my every move.

I needed to get a job and get out of the house, partly to help pay the bills and partly to get away from Jeff. So, I began waitressing at the local mall. The work was exhausting, both physically and mentally. I resented having to work full time while

Jeff was home all-day watching television and playing with Kevin. It took him six months to find a new job, but he didn't appear happy or grateful about it. I think he had grown accustomed to his comfortable, stay-at-home lifestyle and liked not having to answer to authority while wearing a suit. He was also a low man on the totem pole again and didn't like having to start all over. But I had faith in him. I *needed* him to succeed at this job. Maybe then, he wouldn't have to drink so much, and he would not be around to make my life so miserable.

Thankfully, Jeff rose to the challenge at his new job. He was up early each day and was usually the first one in the office. He even stayed late when he had to. Jeff reveled in the camaraderie of a "team" again. Around the water cooler, he was always the first to bring up last night's Yankees or Giants game and knew all the details of each play. He also had a soft shoulder to cry on if someone had a personal problem.

Yet despite this confident façade, he was plagued by self-doubt. "Am I good enough to be in this job?" he would constantly ask. I encouraged him to believe in himself. And even though he still drank, I ignored it. Clearly, he was working hard and needed to unwind. Kevin was four years old when he got chicken pox. Since Jeff had never had them as a child, he too was soon infected. He lay in bed for four days, complaining loudly and miserably, scratching the welts that covered his body. I tried to be sympathetic, but I was frustrated because he was at home and helpless—again. After two weeks, he was back to work and right back to his drinking.

One Sunday morning during a snow storm in February, shortly after Jeff had had the chicken pox, we were in the middle of another heated argument about his drinking. I had begun to contemplate leaving him but hadn't been able to deal with the reality of doing so. Our shouting was interrupted by a phone call. One of Jeff's buddies wanted to see if Jeff wanted to play touch football. I seethed while listening to Jeff, who had suddenly become so animated and friendly with his friend on the phone. "Sure!" He laughed. He was always up for a good pummeling in the snow. He couldn't get away from me fast enough.

He quickly changed into his sweats and sneakers and bolted out the door. I was furious. First, that he was so eager to avoid talking to me, and second because he was risking getting hurt in such messy conditions. Twenty minutes later, the phone rang again. Sure enough, his friend told me that Jeff had blown out his knee. I thought for a moment that I should leave him where he was and let him get home alone, but my mothering instincts got the better of me. I reached for my keys but froze when I realized the horror of the situation: Jeff would be out of commission again and would have to be at home. When I picked him up at the field, he was in agony but refused to go to the emergency room. He hobbled into the house, and, like a dog licking his wounds, he retreated to the basement with a six-pack of beer to numb his pain. The next day, the doctor recommended immediate surgery. Jeff was admitted to the hospital and prepped. His blood work showed that he had dangerously high blood pressure; he was a heart attack waiting to happen.

Before they could operate, they needed to stabilize his blood pressure. Days later, when he was finally operated on, the orthopedist discovered that Jeff's knee required more complicated surgery. He spent a week recovering in the hospital, then came home with a prescription for Percocet in his pocket and a cast up to his thigh. Beer was all he needed to toss down his pills. Would I be kind enough to get him one? And, of course, being his number-one enabler, I did.

During his convalescence, he became more isolated and depressed. He couldn't go to work. He couldn't take a shower or get around by himself. There was nothing I could do to ease his anxiety while he lay in bed, helplessly watching the days pass by. But he appreciated all of my help with his most basic needs and thanked me profusely each and every day, which was my only consolation. In the end, he needed weeks and weeks of rehabilitation and missed several months of work. Unfortunately, all of this isolation and time off allowed him to nurture his blossoming addiction.

At home, we were like two bulls locked in battle. He refused to admit that his drinking was destroying our lives. I refused to give up my mission to save him and our marriage. Sometimes after a bitter argument, he would storm out the door, get in the car, and drive around for hours to calm down. These sudden, angry departures scared me. Was he drunk again? Was he jeopardizing other people's lives by driving? Would he ever come home again?

I thought that if Jeff got the perfect job, we had a second child, and he fixed his knee and exercised, the problems would all go away—that all would be OK. I wasn't even looking for perfection, just not this constant chaos, stress, and dissension. Now I see that no matter what was right or wrong in our lives, alcohol was the reason.

It stood alone; nothing could have made our lives better or worse with this disease. Hadn't we suffered indignities enough? Been criticized and humiliated way beyond our faults? I felt abandoned and betrayed when the disease continued. And then came the disappointment. He had his arms wrapped around the bottle, and I had my arms wrapped around Jeff. I realized my life was unmanageable, but I didn't think I was powerless. I thought that if I could protect him from the adversities of life, the better he would be able to cope and, therefore, not drink. My well-intentioned motives always fell flat. Although I failed miserably and was very discouraged, I thought next time would be different if only I could have another crack at it. We were so enmeshed with each other that I became intrusive and interfering. In our desperation, we picked at each other until every scrap of love and trust was destroyed. I listened sympathetically to his tales of woe as we denied, ignored, and argued over what was really wrong with our lives.

The phrase "hurt people hurt people" explained that even though we loved each other, we unwittingly continued the destructive cycle of negative attitudes and abusive behavior, although we desired to act differently. We both wanted to get rid of the pain. Blame, guilt, anger, depression, and many other negative attitudes already had gone on for generations in our families affected by alcoholism.

I was already overburdened with taking too much responsibility for Jeff's unpredictable behavior. I would shake my head vehemently. "Wrong! I am not crazy. I saw you take that bottle into the basement, and now I want you to give it to me!"

I was flabbergasted and reacted defensively at his nasty comments when he attempted to joke about it. Alcoholism can turn triumph into tragedy and love into grim determination. He pushed all my buttons. I looked pensive and bemused as he retrieved his secret stash. Did I really need to be right about this, though? I didn't feel relieved, just sick and worried.

I thought, over and over, *there's something wrong with this picture.* As the drinking progressed, Jeff's alcohol-induced ranting would continue into late evening. The weekends were the worst: he'd come home cranky from work, start to unwind by drinking, and then feel lousy and depressed about himself and drink some more. If we didn't get into an argument Friday night, it would happen soon after; if I questioned him or didn't pay enough attention, someone or something else would irritate him.

I was afraid to discuss anything sensitive with him anymore. Clearly, he felt vulnerable when any of his emotional inadequacies surfaced. I wanted to avoid all subjects that might provide potential excuses for him to drink. The only thing I could predict about Jeff was his unpredictability. He could be sweet as molasses one minute and dark as a thunderhead the next. And if I ever tried to talk to him when he was drunk and in one of his dark moods, he would shut down and become uncommunicative. Later, when he was temporarily sober, he would apologize and tell me how much he loved me with a kiss on the forehead as he headed to work as though nothing had happened. He promised it would never happen again. I hated being married.

Even little Kevin was not immune to Jeff's erratic mood swings. Once, when he was four years old, and they were kicking the soccer ball around in the backyard, Kevin came into the house crying, "Daddy won't let me kick the ball. He keeps telling me what to do." I told Jeff to go easy on him and let him have the ball; he was just a little kid, for goodness' sake. Jeff just looked at me with a disdainful stare. He insisted that Kevin needed to learn the game's rules and play fair.

He sounded ridiculous and overly harsh, and I wasn't afraid to tell him. It appeared that I was taking sides. I was meddling again. I could see Jeff's anger beginning to boil over. He shouted back that I was babying Kevin and to butt out. He was going to teach him how to play soccer the right way. Kevin just cried louder and ran from the room, fearful of his father's booming voice.

Jeff continued to try to run from his demons, too. Two months after his knee surgery, Kevin had a music concert at school. Jeff hobbled into the auditorium on crutches. He had spent half the night awake because of the terrible itching under his cast.

As we sat side by side listening to the concert, I could smell Jeff's alcohol breath. I was disgusted and embarrassed. What if someone else detected that he was drinking during the day? Later I confronted Jeff about drinking before the concert. I was sure he was drunk, even though I had no physical proof. He told me I was crazy, that I didn't know what I was talking about. Then he stormed upstairs. Minutes later, he appeared in the kitchen, holding a packed suitcase in one hand and five-year-old Kevin in the other. "Where are you going?" I asked, dumbstruck.

"I'm taking Kevin and leaving," he said. "You don't believe or trust me anyway."

I would have been ecstatic had he walked out the door at that moment. But he was holding little Kevin, and I couldn't risk having Jeff take him away from me and possibly jeopardizing his life. Jeff was like a crazed animal. He had a sick, almost maniacal look on his face. He seemed to enjoy that he was tearing my heart in half and that he could wield such power over me. I pleaded with him to stay because I was afraid for Kevin. I had made Jeff angry because I had confronted him about his breath. If only I was good, he wouldn't take my baby away from me. I learned my lesson: always have the evidence in hand.

Jeff's knee surgery was a turning point in his destructive spiral. During his recuperation, he had plenty of time—more time than he cared to have—

to think about the many things in his life that he had done wrong or the poor choices he had made. He thought about his childhood, too, and the sorrow that he had bottled up over the years. It was as if the wound on his knee healed while a whole new wound opened in his heart. This wound had festered below the surface for his entire life, and, like slow-growing cancer, it had finally become visible.

Jeff had grown up in Orange, New Jersey. He had a sister four years younger. His mom was a teacher at a prestigious school but a closet drinker who kept her blackberry brandy hidden in her underwear drawer. She was controlling, imperious, and distant. Nothing was ever good enough for her. When Jeff came home with an A on his report card, she would ask, "Why didn't you get an A-plus?" Jeff felt like he could never live up to his mother's impossible expectations.

And like Jeff, I never felt I could live up to my father's. It was as if the gods had conspired to bring our two wounded souls together, bringing our two negative pasts into one flaming, dysfunctional present. We were "damaged goods" whose attraction was cosmic. Jeff's dad was a probation officer who ruled his home like the law-enforcer that he was. He was often sullen, uncommunicative, and prone to violent outbursts. He had little patience for Jeff and his sister's typical childhood antics. Although Jeff never spoke to me about his childhood, he once told me about the time his dad hit him repeatedly for doing nothing when he was only five years old. I often wonder now how many more beatings were buried somewhere in Jeff's tangled memories. Were these memories what ultimately festered and poisoned Jeff's consciousness?

As an adult, Jeff shared little with his dad. When they were in the same room, the tension was palpable. Nothing too controversial was ever spoken. Jeff's dad had always had a superficial relationship with him, so it was nothing out of the ordinary for him to talk about the weather, old acquaintances, or his days as a parole officer. Luckily for Jeff, when we married, I created another layer of distance between Jeff and his dad. He would no longer have to speak to his dad one on one. He could speak to his dad *through* me. And this was just fine with Jeff.

Even though Jeff had no latent awareness of his abuse, the effects of his childhood still plagued him as an adult. The core of his difficulties included an inability to trust, low self-esteem, depression, relationship problems, and alcohol. The emotional abandonment left him in a painful and depressed state. He lacked consistent nurturing, protection, and guidance. This made for internal deprivation, emptiness, and isolation. He tried to fill the emptiness, to replace the love and security, with a temporary respite from the pain. He was compelled to keep drinking; he literally could not stop himself. It had probably started as a way to distract himself from the pain of his parents, numbing his loneliness and isolation, and then became an obsession.

We saw his father and stepmom on special occasions—holidays and birthdays only. My mother-in-law would periodically phone and ask, "Why doesn't Jeff pay any attention to his father?" I was the messenger caught in the middle. Puzzled, I asked Jeff why he didn't ever see his father; he lived so close, but they never got together.

He snapped, "It's none of your business. I don't need to be told what to do when it's my dad."

This was very true; it really was absolutely none of my business. I reminded him, "I'm only relaying what I was asked to. Don't shoot the messenger."

Jeff's knee surgery also guaranteed that he would never play sports again, which was another major turning point in the acceleration of his disease. No longer would he be able to slam the tennis ball around the court or go out for a jog. He limped and began to put on weight. There was no place to take out his energy or get rid of the bad feelings about himself. This was another reason to drink more. It was during this post-surgery period that it seemed as if the weight of the world had come crashing down upon Jeff. Our fertility failures, his loss of mobility, his absences from work, and our mounting resentment toward each other made drinking the only bright spot in his otherwise complicated and disappointing life. By now, his love affair with alcohol was in full swing.

When Kevin was two years old, we started trying to have another child. Since getting pregnant with Kevin was so easy, I assumed this time would be the same but to no avail. Jeff felt inadequate and depressed even more.

Between tearing his ACL, arthroscopic and reconstructive surgery, and a cast on his entire leg, his depression major was understandable. He gave up on rehabilitation too early, so after going through all this, his knee didn't heal properly, and he walked with a limp. It was an awful time between this injury, fertility issues, and job losses.

For 5 ½ years, we were tortured with doctor appointments, minor surgeries, and huge medical bills. I injected myself with my stomach fat for 4 years with Clomid. Then I moved on to a large needle injection of Pergonal in my rear end for another year. I visited a fertility clinic in a hospital in Newark, New Jersey, every month. And every month was a huge disappointment when I wasn't pregnant. There was a time when we were very close to adopting a Korean baby. And finally, we tried another avenue with success. The one sunny moment during this time was when we found out I was finally pregnant again. After five years, we were so happy and relieved. Unfortunately, the happiness was short-lived. Jeff came home soon after and announced he had lost his job. Evidently, people at work had been talking about his drinking. Someone had complained to management that he smelled like alcohol. When I asked him if he had, in fact, been drinking, he denied it. I didn't believe him. He complained that his company had no proof that he was drinking. He felt that he had been treated unfairly. Secretly, I sensed that he was relieved not to have to go to work. Now he had all the time in the world again to drink in peace and quiet at home. But now, I would have to suffer from him lying around the house again.

There were bills to be paid and mouths to feed, so I returned to work at the restaurant full time, grumbling each day about having to work while he had the luxury of staying at home. I was sick and tired, not only from being pregnant but from Jeff's lack of responsibility. *If he hadn't been such a drinker, I wouldn't be waiting tables*, I thought. At night I would come home and dive into bed. My very pregnant body ached all over. He was unemployed for over a year; it was difficult making ends meet. However, during that time, he was a fabulous dad and enjoyed doing everything for and with Kevin. Nothing was too "dorky" if it was about his towheaded son.

But there was another silver lining to Jeff's unemployment. It appeared that he had gotten his drinking under control (or perhaps, because I wasn't home during the day, I didn't see it). Maybe it was because he had picked up a few jobs helping a friend paint house. Being stone-cold drunk on a ladder wasn't Jeff's idea of a fun buzz. Besides, he was invigorated by being outside, and he liked the hard work.

As winter approached and the prospect of working outdoors appeared less appealing, Jeff yearned to get back to corporate life. But six months had passed, and still, there were no job offers on the table.

When I was seven months pregnant, we took a trip to Disney World. It would be our one last fling as a family of three before the new baby arrived. Everything was perfect—until I woke up one morning in the hotel to find that Jeff was missing.

"Where's daddy?" Kevin asked over and over again.

"He's taking a walk," I said.

After three hours, Kevin had lost his patience. "Why is daddy taking such a long walk?" he cried. The pit in my stomach tightened. I knew Jeff was up to no good.

After another hour, I heard the key turn in the lock. As the door slowly opened, I could smell the stench of alcohol waft into the room. "Where have you been?" I calmly inquired.

"It's none of your business! You are such a nag! I wasn't drinking, and I hate you for accusing me of that again!" he screamed.

"OK, I made a mistake; I was wrong to say anything. I just want to have a nice vacation! I'm sorry!" I begged on my knees.

"Well, forget it. I'm taking Kevin and going home. You can stay here by yourself!"

I collapsed in tears, begging him to forgive me, not take Kevin and leave and try to forget I said anything.

Again, I had no proof that he was drinking. I just had my well-trained nose and my gut instinct to tell me. After that, I regretted saying anything. I shouldn't have ruined our otherwise idyllic vacation by arguing about his drinking. The next day, we flew home. We rarely traveled together as a family again.

Two months later, on May 13, 1993, our daughter, Kelsey Anne, was born. When I went into labor, the first thing Jeff did was down a couple of beers. He powered through my labor, staying up all night with me until she was born the next morning. Jeff fell in love with Kelsey the moment she was placed in his arms. He had that same look of perfect bliss written across his face. When we arrived home from the hospital, my neighbor took a picture of the four of us. We looked like the perfect family sitting on the front step. I wanted the moment to last forever because I knew life would soon return to our old, normal routine dominated by Jeff's drinking. But Jeff proved himself to be a trouper once again, changing diapers, making bottles, and getting up in the middle of the night so I could sleep. It was hard to believe that he was such a good dad with such a bad drinking problem.

Kevin was a wonderful big brother and was very protective of his baby sister, Kelsey. They were seven years apart in age, but we still went to visit friends in Vermont every winter, and he skied the mountain while she stayed on the bunny slope. We still went to the beach together every day during July and August while Kevin surfed the big waves and Kelsey sold handmade friendship bracelets and beaded necklaces. Jeff adored his children. He always took over when he came in from work or arrived in Lavallette for the weekend. He would whisk either one of them up in his arms and sing Bob Seeger songs to them. Or he would hold them in his lap and strum the guitar and sing out of tune to amuse them. When they were babies, he would insist on changing them and picking out a nice outfit that would give him great pleasure. I always appreciated him and would gladly give him time with them since he was a good dad. I spent part of the summers with the kids in Lavallette. It was a much-needed break from Jeff's constant rumination about his miserable life and why he needed another drink. When he did come for weekends and vacation weeks, we enjoyed each other's company with the kids. The anticipation of the shore after the long winter was everywhere. The season is so short that everyone is ready to hit the beach on Memorial Day weekend and continue throughout the summer months into September. Jeff enjoyed crabbing and swimming with Kevin.

For a while, tensions at home lessened. Jeff got a new job, and I was able to stay home with the kids. It appeared that he had gotten his drinking under control again and was enjoying life. During this time, he loved being a dad. He would offer to stay home with the kids when they were napping if I wanted to get out. Sometimes I went to the beach or shopping when he was home at night or on weekends. When Kelsey was eager to go out with me, Jeff would convince her to stay with promises of playing games or watching a video (which he always followed through with). She was his "petunia" as he watched *Spongebob Squarepants* and *Mister Rogers' Neighborhood* with her. As she got older and wanted to dust or knit or paint with me, he called her "mini-mom."

He taught Kevin how to play the guitar, instilling in him a love of music he still has today. Jeff could play every song by Jackson Browne, the Eagles, and Chicago well. The two of them constantly talked about sports. Jeff was a passionate Raiders fan, and Kevin a Giants fan. During games, they were like rabid fans screaming at the TV. Sports were Jeff's release—even when he only sat on the couch and watched. His nicknames for Kevin varied between "geezer" and "geez boy."

Between bouts of drinking, Jeff was a true comic. He often joked that he would love to do a cynical, sarcastic stand-up routine. His sheer genius sense of humor could break up a tense moment. When Kevin was a baby, Jeff found one of his booties lodged in his dress shirt at work one day. He reached for it and made some funny remark. He had a natural, fun-loving way of connecting with people, whether they were older, younger, or his contemporaries. Sadly, as the years passed, this side of Jeff's personality showed itself less and less frequently. There was no way we could have foreseen the demons he would unleash in the years to come. I thought we could finally be happy. Jeff had a good job, we had two beautiful children, and we had a semi-truce between us. But nothing ever really made our lives click; nothing external made my alcoholic husband like his life except alcohol.

Chapter 10: Hopeless

During the middle years of our marriage, Jeff became a professional alcoholic. Not only did his taste for alcohol become more sophisticated, but his ability to hide his addiction became more adept. He would ask me to buy tonic water at the grocery store, and I, being so naïve, blindly bought it for him, not realizing that he was now using it to mix with hard liquor.

Kelsey was two when I noticed that he began to sip all day long from a large tumbler. He carried it with him from room to room and kept it near his side. He had never sipped or carried a beer around the house like that before. Why was he suddenly so thirsty? Why was he so concerned about keeping that cup near him? I believed he was concealing his drinking, but I desperately needed to find evidence to support my suspicions.

Then I would have proof! Yes, his secret would no longer be his. I would have something to hold over him. He would no longer control me with his drinking. Everything would be out in the open, and we could finally deal with his addiction. My desire to feel control over his drinking was one way I could make sense of our dysfunctional relationship. He lied to me constantly—which was almost worse than the drinking itself—and I didn't trust him. Now we were constantly fighting. Our relationship became an endless game of cat and mouse, with me trying to figure out his next move and him always managing to elude me. This was no way to exist as husband and wife, much less as a family. I felt like my life was spiraling out of control and that I needed to break the vicious cycle to get it back. I would have to wait for just the right moment, though before I could confirm my suspicions.

One morning, around 6:00 a.m., I woke up early and heard Jeff shuffling about downstairs, listening to the morning news on the TV. When I heard him close the bathroom door, I knew I had my chance. Quickly, I crept downstairs. I saw the drink sitting on the table next to his favorite recliner and moved closer. I took a sip and almost gagged. That was one stiff gin and tonic! I turned and quietly climbed back into bed. But I lay there for a long time, stunned. My worst fears were confirmed. Jeff had now progressed to drinking hard liquor.

That morning, I thought about all the reasons I should leave Jeff. I had a comfortable nest egg. I owned the house. It would be tough, I thought, but I could go back to work and raise the kids myself. Yet somehow, my own inner demons had a way of twisting the reality of the situation. If I just stuck it out, my bruised heart reasoned, maybe I could make Jeff change. Maybe I could have that perfect family someday. I could make up for my lost childhood. *I did love him, didn't I?* And he wasn't beating me. With such limited contact with the few members of our families that were still alive, *we* were all we had. I would make things work—for me, for us, and for the kids. I was fiercely determined to protect our family unit. Somehow, I believed that if I just worked harder, things would improve.

Later that night, after I had found the gin and tonic, I confronted Jeff about it. His face turned pale. "Sandy," he said, "I'm sorry. You know I love you."

"If you truly wanted this marriage to work with me," I said, "you would stop drinking."

"I'll stop," he promised. "This time, I swear to you, I will."

I had heard enough of his empty promises. This was my moment to drop my bombshell. "Jeff." I hesitated. "I've been thinking about leaving you."

Jeff sat on the edge of the bed. He was silent. His head dropped into his hands. He looked completely defeated. "Please...Sandy...please don't leave me!" He whispered, "I know I have a problem, I can fix this, but I need you to stick by me."

"What if I can't deal with you anymore?" I shot back. "You have lied to me over and over again about getting help. You are sick, sick, *sick!*"

"Please," he whispered. "Just give me some time. I can lick this."

I rolled my eyes. Who was he kidding, thinking he could just stop on his own?

"You need to get into rehab, Jeff. Your drinking is ruining you," I repeated. He wasn't ready to admit this, but maybe saying it in those terms would force him to confront the depths of his addiction.

But there were other, equally troubling signs that Jeff's addiction was consuming his daily life. Once, I watched him hide a gallon of gin in a snow bank on my neighbor's driveway. As soon as he left the house, I took the bottle out of the snow and returned it to the liquor store. To this day, I wonder what his face must have looked like when he went back to get his bottle and found that it was missing. To anyone else, finding a bottle of gin in a snow bank and returning it to a liquor store would be considered bizarre, but through my distorted prism, it seemed like a perfectly normal thing to do.

Later, acting on a hunch, I looked inside the basement ceiling tiles and found about six or seven empty gallon gin jugs. I was completely taken aback at the sheer volume of liquor he had consumed. I took the bottles and placed them in the recycling bin. When he found them, he was livid. "Do you want everyone in the neighborhood to know I drink?" he bellowed.

"I stopped caring who knew a while ago," I said matter-of-factly.

I knew Jeff needed help—fast. But he was still so stubborn about admitting that he had a problem. When I suggested he try Alcoholics Anonymous, he told me that it was for people with real drinking problems. His drinking was more "situational," he said.

He would come home from work, make himself a drink, and head down to the basement. There in the dim light, he would watch TV and sip gin until he knew I was asleep, then stumble into bed. Every morning he would be apologetic about the night before. Sometimes he even cried as he tried to explain away another night of drunkenness. Again he begged, "I don't know what's wrong with me! Please just give me one more chance to do better? I promise this won't happen again! Please stick by me! I need you and the kids so much. I can't stand the thought of losing you!"

Jeff thought maybe we should take a trip with the kids to Sanibel Island, Florida. That would help us put things back together, he reasoned. I refused to go. The thought of being cooped up in a hotel room with him made me sick. If I was going anywhere, it would be to a support group for alcoholics. I picked up the phone book and found the listing for AA. A kind man on the other end of the phone listened as I told him about Jeff's history. He understood completely and didn't make me feel embarrassed. He agreed that Jeff's situation was serious—that he needed to get into a rehab unit soon. There, he could dry out with medical supervision and with the help of detox medications. This sounded like the first sensible plan that had come our way. I made phone calls. I inquired about rehab facilities in our area. I gathered all of my facts.

Later that night, after the kids were asleep, I approached Jeff. "You are going to kill yourself if you don't stop drinking," I told him.

Jeff didn't want to hear any of it. "I don't need any stinkin' doctors to help me stop drinking!" he shouted. "I can do it myself!" He slammed the door and went back down to the basement, where he spent the night.

During this period, I suggested to him that he drink a soda or water instead of a beer. "You're nothing but a nag," he bellowed from the basement.

So, Jeff devised his own method of detoxing. He spent the next four days locked in the spare bedroom and went cold turkey. He only came out to use the bathroom. He was clearly in agony, shaking, writhing, and sweating profusely in the bed. He couldn't stomach the thought of food but oddly was able to eat an entire five-pound bag of sugar over the course of the four days while alcohol oozed from his pores. When he finally went back to work, he told his coworkers that he had a bad case of the flu. Jeff was ecstatic. He felt he had slain the dragon. He believed he had cured himself. I wasn't so sure.

Soon, Jeff began to develop bouts of severe abdominal pain. He would be doubled over, lying on the bathroom floor, and made me call in sick for him. Then he would tell me to go away. He just wanted to be left alone, he said. I suspected that he had begun drinking again. When I asked, he'd scream at me again; it was none of my business what he was doing. These bouts of abdominal pain seemed to come and go like the weather. Sometimes he would come home from work at 11:00 a.m. Sometimes he would wake up in pain in the middle of the night. He could be sick for a day or for days on end. There was no pattern to his pain.

I sought help from Jeff's sister. Pouring my heart out to her, I described how desperate I had become about Jeff's drinking. She knew her brother well. She felt strongly that his drinking was situational, that he was merely drinking because of some unfortunate turns in his life. He was clearly able to control it (he had stopped on more than one occasion, right?). She suggested we map out a plan: Jeff could drink one glass of beer or wine at dinner and only in front of me. Then we discussed seeing a therapist. I knew in my heart that *I* needed to see one. I was sure Jeff would fight it, though. To him, asking for help constituted weakness. Remember, he believed he was able to control his drinking. He didn't need anyone's help!

After several job changes and years of drinking, the effects of the disease began to take a heavy toll. My compulsive thinking made it impossible to keep up the act of cheerfulness, and my sunny disposition was replaced by anger and the silent treatment. Alcoholism is a disease. Nobody wants to be afflicted by it, and we didn't either—not Jeff, not me.

I reached out to Al-Anon. I sat and listened to others share their experiences, strength, and hope, and suddenly the events of all those years had a context and an explanation. I had already spent most of my adult life alternating between hiding from the truth and trying to force a solution. My fear of repeating history for another generation outweighed the fear of exposing the disease. Nevertheless, it still took time for me to feel better; knowing more about alcoholism did not magically erase the effects it had had on me. I had to take down the "everything's fine" façade. Worst of all, I began to reveal family secrets that we had ignored forever. Speaking out for myself changed my perception of myself. I was no longer terribly shy and quiet as I received validation for my courage to tell my story.

I felt exhausted trying to manage everything and realized I didn't have to. At a meeting, I heard a statement that changed my life: "He doesn't have to be comfortable." When I stopped taking responsibility for my husband's feelings, I allowed him to experience the consequences of his behavior and feel his own discomfort. I hoped this discomfort would lead Jeff to seek sobriety. He had so much self-hatred, remorse, and guilt; he felt useless and worthless. Instead, he got worse, and during the incredibly painful process of separation, Al-Anon stood like a beacon flashing in the darkness, shedding light, comfort, hope, and strength.

What I couldn't see at that time was how Jeff's stubborn denial kept him from ever being able to face his demons enough to get help. I didn't know how insidious the disease of alcoholism was. Through my friends at Al-Anon, I found that alcoholism is like a vicious catch-22. The alcoholic needs to admit he needs help but can't because he's an alcoholic. He lives behind a veil of lies and deceit. Jeff fit the classic profile: his drinking had affected every aspect of his life—from his marriage to his relationship with his children to his friendships to his ability to hold a job. When he returned from an errand, we argued as usual.

He uttered those familiar words, "This isn't working. I think we should call it quits."

I rolled my eyes and interrupted him, "Make up your mind! One day you want out, the next you want to work on the marriage." I shared this with painful honesty and thought he really meant that he wanted out this time. There was no reasoning with him. I wanted to bolt from the room. I had that sinking feeling in the pit of my stomach: fear. The lead weight on my chest some mornings was anguish and discontent with dread for the day, that cold lump in the center of myself that said I was wrong for staying, wrong to leave.

"I consider divorce a failure, and I don't want to give up," Jeff said.

I gritted my teeth and replied, "That's easy for you to say; you're causing all the problems!" My heart pounded. Standing my ground was a tremendously bold action for me. I always wanted him to succeed, to be happy, to know that I cared.

He pulled out all the stops. "I'll take the kids away from you if you even try to leave me." He knew my weaknesses well and jabbed at every emotional hot button I had. I winced and remained silent, but I couldn't quell the rising panic I felt.

Then I snapped and shouted, "You're driving me crazy. Are you happy now? I am going insane! I am nuts! It's not my fault you can't hold down a job and can't stop drinking! I can't live like this any longer!"

The things I swore I would never do, I did. Things that had gone on in my house when I was growing up now happened in my own home.

"Doesn't divorce cost a lot of money?" He asked, hoping for an out. I kept quiet. There was nothing more to say.

Again, I felt the terror those words always triggered. This time, I knew better than to beg him to stay; I wanted him to leave. I was sick of my life with him and his huge problems with his father and alcohol abuse. It was painful to dredge up those old memories and feel again the darkest, most distressing things happening. His wounds were not visible, but they were real. He was unable to help himself. He overreacted to simple things, and I realized these were "triggers" from the past that he was still traumatized. The deepest grief was that I watched Jeff's soul die a little more each day because of the pain he carried. It was so hard to let go when everything inside me said, *Hang on tighter.*

I scolded, cajoled, and tried everything to make him stop the drinking that was ruining his family, career, and health. Of course, nothing worked since he would not admit that he had a serious problem with alcohol. Only he could come to the realization that he had a progressive disease that could eventually end in his death. I gave him love, understanding, and support, but I couldn't stop his drinking. I didn't understand or label it for the first few years. I was astonished that he couldn't see that this was wrong. Why couldn't he just resist temptation, relax, and do something to stop it! I was obsessed with my husband's problems. My mission was to get him sober before he ruined everything, and I honestly believed I could do it.

Despite my urging that he stop drinking, I continued to find empty bottles and cans hidden in coat pockets, holes in the garage or basement, behind walls, and in his briefcase. Jeff didn't care what he drank now.

He might start with gin and finish with beer or drink a bottle of wine and cap it off with straight gin. Always, after I found the hard evidence, he denied that the bottles and cans were even his. He would glare at me bitterly, purse his lips and shout, "You've made a mistake. Your imagination is running wild, Sandy. You're crazy!"

I would shout back, "What are you talking about? Who else could they be? No one else drinks around here but you!"

"Never mind," Jeff said sternly. He'd storm out of the room in the middle of a sentence.

I just waited for him to pass out on the couch so we could relax for the evening. Invariably, it would end with the same refrain from Jeff. "I just had a beer or two, and I promise it won't happen again. Don't be upset. I love you and the kids. I'm going to make things right!"

I threatened that I would walk out the door if he didn't agree to get help. Finally, he agreed— although only to see a marriage counselor. During the sessions, Jeff wanted to know why I would want to stay with him if all he did was cause me trouble. He was afraid I was going to leave him. The counselor assured him that I was staying because I loved him and wanted to work out our problems.

But after just three sessions, Jeff balked about going. He went reluctantly to the fourth session, but that night, the doctor suggested that perhaps his poor relationship with his mother might be the cause of some of his depression. This struck a raw nerve. Jeff railed against the doctor as we were leaving. "What does he know about my mother? He has no right to tell me that I'm like her!" I had never heard him say a nice word about her before. I was dumbfounded that he would feel the need to defend her now. Needless to say, that was the last night we went to couples therapy.

I found a new therapist for myself and continued to reach out to Al-Anon to find more answers and get some peace. Unfortunately, Jeff was listening in on the conversation when I scheduled the appointment for the therapist. He wanted to know why I would need to talk to someone about us. Was I going to tell them all about his problems? He didn't want me telling some stranger our deepest secrets. But Jeff had bullied me again into thinking what I was doing was wrong. So, I called back to cancel the appointment. Then, confusing me further, a few days later, he said, "Go ahead, talk to someone if you think it will make you feel better." So, I went.

The therapist immediately realized that I had to establish some boundaries with Jeff. We talked about Jeff's alcoholism during every session, but I, being afraid to confront the real issues, talked so much about Jeff's positive qualities, instead of the horror of our disagreements, that the therapist didn't agree that I really wanted to leave the marriage. My ability to stand up for myself was still shaky at this point.

How was I going to get Jeff to stop drinking? I was totally obsessed. I was constantly on the lookout for signs that he was drinking or even thinking about it. I felt the need to distract him, keep him happy so he wouldn't remember to drink. I first went to Al-Anon to get someone to tell me how to stop him from self-destruction. I wanted to straighten him out, make him see the light. I was naïve to think that I could fix, change, or control anything about this. I was overwhelmed, frazzled, and weary as I waited anxiously for him to leave, then anticipated him coming home. He wasn't fond of being told what to do. He "managed" to keep his drinking under some kind of "control" when he needed to but didn't participate in life.

In Al-Anon, I was listened to without interruption. Still, I resisted. I was skeptical. Meetings reduced my isolation and the sinking feeling that I was again alone with the problems that go hand in hand with alcoholism. It provided a new perspective on a difficult situation when I felt attacked or rejected. It straightened out my obsessive thinking and calmed my fears. I stayed in the moment, or at least the day, and didn't project into a doom-and-gloom future. The short version of the first three steps is, "I can't. God can. Let him." One day I realized that the fear that used to have total power over me was receding as I chiseled away at the unpleasant feelings and excruciating grief at the idea of leaving Jeff.

Finally, I saturated myself in the recovery program, which focused on my codependency. The security of being around others who had been in similar situations was comforting. For the first time, I was getting some answers and began to feel like I was not crazy. At first, I had to sneak off to meetings because I was afraid Jeff would intimidate me. When he finally did find out, he said I was making a huge production out of nothing. (Again, his blatant denials were huge red flags.) He was constantly trying to define my reality for me by telling me how I should feel and what I should see and know. I got information about conducting an intervention. But I was too afraid of living with the aftermath. I was sure no one would even believe me, of course, because Jeff was such a nice person to the outside world.

Jeff and I held deep variations on the theme of alcoholism and abuse from our families of origin. Jeff was addicted to alcohol, and I was addicted to him. We were kindred spirits, again linked together by some cosmic connection. As I dug deep down into the trenches of my own childhood, I became aware of the bond that existed between us. God had intended us to be together. He doesn't make mistakes. It would be difficult to tear apart what was so deeply entwined.

Meanwhile, I had been trying to shield my children from the worst of Jeff's behavior, but our constant screaming matches made it impossible to contain the disaster that was unfolding before them. Kelsey told me one evening, "Daddy used my favorite cup and poured wine into it; he shouldn't do that." She had watched him from the kitchen. Obviously, he hadn't known she was there, or he would not have used it. Angrily I told him to clean up his act, or I was through with him. I explained how pitiful it was that his six-year-old daughter knew he had a drinking problem.

"You make me sick!" I screamed.

He was mortified. "I'm so sorry, it'll never happen again. I love my family so much; I don't want to lose you!" Again, more of the same empty promises.

The children knew to run when our words began to erupt. It broke my heart to see them cower or hide in their rooms whenever we fought. This was not the kind of example I had ever wanted to set for my children. But it was our reality, and I did my best to make them feel secure and loved. I would talk to them afterward to gauge how they were feeling. I tried to keep them busy with their regular activities. I worked hard to keep a semblance of normality in their day by serving their favorite dinners and taking them to movies. But they knew I was desperate. They saw my tears and heard my anguished cries. I began to feel that I needed to save them from this hell of an existence. I was afraid, sure. But I also owed it to my children to protect them from our arguing.

Once, they watched in captive horror as Jeff verbally abused and threatened me. It happened one night while the four of us were driving down the parkway to visit some friends. Another driver, presumably angry at Jeff's driving, passed us. Jeff went ballistic, yelling at the driver and speeding up to confront him. I told him to calm down, the kids were in the car, and I didn't want to get into an accident. Jeff was livid. He pulled into a parking lot and slammed the car to a stop.

"Don't you ever tell me what to do when I drive!" he shouted. He pounded the steering wheel. "Just keep your mouth shut from now on. I don't need your advice!"

Then he pointed his finger right in my face. "Stop talking to me about my drinking every day; I don't want your help!"

By now, the kids were crying in the back seat. I begged him to stop. I couldn't let the kids suffer through this.

"I'm sorry," I whimpered, "you win. I'll do whatever you want! I promise I won't talk about your drinking again."

This made him even angrier. What was I to do? We were in the middle of nowhere. He was behind the wheel, and we were at his mercy. I wanted to go home. I wanted to get as far away from him as I could. After twenty minutes, he put the car into drive and continued down the highway, silent and seething under his breath. I shook the rest of the way there, too afraid to ask him to turn around. When we walked in the door of our friend's house, it took all my strength to act like nothing had happened. It stung to think we were just like my parents, acting like we were the perfect family when we arrived for the holidays. Jeff took me aside and tried to apologize over and over again. But the damage was done. I was afraid of him and his outbursts. He had risked all of our lives.

I knew it was time to make plans to leave my marriage.

The next week, I saw a divorce lawyer to find out what my financial rights were. She was completely sympathetic and understood my situation. She had dealt with women who were abused all the time and knew I spoke the truth. For the first time in a long time, I felt safe—and sane. She gave me some papers to fill out and told me to think about what I wanted to do. I could come back when I was certain. I tucked the papers in the cabinet in the dining room under a bunch of books.

Later that weekend, Jeff was rifling through the cabinet searching for something and came across the papers. He held them up and chased me through the house.

"What are you doing?" he shouted. "Do you really think you're going to leave me?" I cowered and reminded him about how he had been so mean to me and how his drinking had ruined our marriage. By now, the veins in his neck were bulging. He shook the papers over my head. "What have I done that is so bad that you run off behind my back and see a divorce lawyer?"

Suddenly, he collapsed on the kitchen counter, crying and begging, "Please don't do this; I'll change; I promise I'll do anything—rehab, therapy—anything to keep you. I can't live without you!"

My heart said *OK*, but my head knew that I shouldn't back down so easily. I should have had him sign a contract to hold him to the promises he made. But I didn't. After that day, he was on his best behavior for a while.

Jeff finally decided to give AA a chance after he knew I wanted to leave him. After his first meeting, he was interested in the program and willing to give it a try—on his terms, though. At the end of one of his first meetings, he mentioned to a few old-timers that he had his son's spring concert at school and wouldn't be at the following night's meeting. They came down on him hard and said, "This is the most important thing you can do for yourself. Skip the concert. You seriously need to be here instead." Jeff didn't like that at all and wasn't going to listen to them. He never went to the concert. Nor did he go to the meeting that night.

With his semi-regular attendance at AA and his new resolve to quit drinking, things began to look up. The depression lifted, his confidence was bolstered, and his morale improved. Jeff was on a new mission to heal himself. He was happier, and for the first time in a long time, he felt in control of his life. I, too, began to have the confidence to move forward. I worked with my new support groups. I came to know that my husband had a physical and chemical addiction to alcohol. It wasn't *him*; it was the disease that was ruining our lives.

The biggest difference in my life after therapy and being in recovery was that I was able to stand up for myself. If we argued now, I would fight back instead of sitting quietly and crying. My new, confident self wouldn't let Jeff talk me down, and I knew it was important for my children to hear me defend myself against his bullying behavior.

Our marriage took a turn for the better. We were getting along. Jeff had a job. He bought a drum set and banged away for hours in the basement every night, teaching himself another song from his teen years. He'd come up from the basement invigorated instead of sad. I was teaching. Maybe we would get through this, after all.

Chapter 11: From Bad to Worse

In April 2004, Kelsey and I went to Florida to visit my sister for spring break. When we arrived home at Newark Airport, I called Jeff on my cell phone to say we had landed. He was supposed to pick us up. There was a long pause before he spoke. "What's wrong?" I asked into the silence on the other end of the phone.

"I ran into the back of a Hummer getting off the highway," Jeff said.

My heart sank. Visions of Jeff drunk behind the wheel came flooding back. "There was a lot of traffic, and I just couldn't stop," he said quietly.

I needed details. Could he have fallen off the wagon and hit the car in a drunken stupor? "Did you call the police and file an accident report?" I asked.

"No," he said. More silence.

The scaffolding of my newly rebuilt life came crashing down. I knew at that moment that Jeff had been drinking again. Why else wouldn't he have reported the accident?

As I approached the baggage claim, I could see Jeff hobbling toward me. My worst suspicions were confirmed. His clothes were disheveled, and I could smell his sour alcohol breath a mile away. I wanted to turn around and run. Couldn't I just get back on another plane to Florida, so I didn't have to deal with the reality of my drunk husband? I needed to be strong and control my anger in front of Kelsey.

We gathered up the luggage and made our way out to the parking garage. I thought it was probably just a simple fender bender, so I brushed off the incident. "It'll be OK," I told him. Then I saw it. The hood of the car was smashed to pieces. This was no minor ding. Now I knew why he didn't want to call the police. My next thought was that this would cost us thousands of dollars to repair. Without a police report, we would not be able to file a claim with our insurance company.

Strangely, I felt a sense of relief that the police weren't involved and that Jeff didn't get a DUI. What legal obstacles would we have faced then? Getting a DUI would have set Jeff back and given him more reason to drink. The accident was easy enough to deal with. Jeff falling off the wagon wasn't.

Later that night, I sat down to talk to Jeff. I could tell he wasn't himself. Maybe it was an accident. But I needed to know what was eating him. What would make him start drinking again?

I asked him, point-blank.

Jeff looked at me cautiously. "While you were away, I had some time to think about many things," he said. "I started to think about when I was a little boy."

I knew Jeff had been tormented by demons from his childhood. But he had never once spoken to me about it. I was eager to listen.

"I remember when I was four or five," he began, his voice wavering, "my father used to beat me."

I could see the tears welling up in his eyes.

I went over and sat next to him. Real tears started to flow. Jeff related to me how something someone had said at an AA meeting triggered a flood of memories about his childhood. He began to remember why he and his dad never had a normal relationship. The pieces of his life's puzzle began to fit together. These memories and deep-seated scars had been buried in the dark recesses of his mind, and now they were resurfacing. Perhaps being alone in the house for four days had given him too much time to dwell on his negative thoughts.

That night, I felt I finally got some answers to the questions that had plagued me throughout our marriage. This explained so much of why Jeff was the way he was. We resolved that night that Jeff would see a counselor specializing in abuse about these new revelations.

But the next day, Jeff was defiant. "Why would I want to see a therapist?" he argued. "I'd rather forget the past."

I felt betrayed, yet again. What more could I do or say that would impact his life? I couldn't trust him to keep a promise. He was sabotaging his own recovery.

The arguments continued. I would try to avoid talking to him altogether, but he constantly badgered me so that I would have no choice but to fight back. Then, no matter what I said, it was the wrong thing.

"Since I never say exactly what you want me to, why don't you just write it down for me, and I'll read it. That would be perfect, Jeff, wouldn't it?" I would say.

Jeff was relentless. His badgering, interrogations, and distrust of my every move made it impossible for me to reason with him. I frequently ended up on my knees, begging him to stop. He seemed to revel in his destructive onslaught. And I, being the good wife, believed it was always my fault.

If he heard me on the phone upstairs, he'd burst into the bedroom. "Why are you talking on the phone in the bedroom and not downstairs?" he would want to know.

I would put my hand over the receiver and motion for him to stop.

"I just want some privacy," I whispered.

"You want privacy? From me? What are you telling people about me?" His face would turn dark. "You think I want to listen to you talk to your friend?"

By now, I would be frantically trying to get off the phone, hoping my girlfriend wouldn't know Jeff was hounding me.

"You're probably going to call that lawyer again—right?" He continued to badger me even after I got off the phone. "If you try to divorce me, you'll be sorry," he threatened.

I pleaded with him. "All I wanted to do was go someplace where it was quiet, and I didn't have to worry about you listening."

"Sandy, I couldn't care less about what you do," he would say with a sneer. He'd purse his lips in angry disapproval if I tried to interject. "Shhhh," he'd hiss.

Then there would be silence. At that moment, I would know the conversation was over, whether I liked it or not. He had put me in my place. Part of me would be relieved that the argument was over, but my adrenaline still surged through my veins. After a few minutes, I'd be trembling with exhaustion, and Jeff, oblivious to what he had just done, would be smiling eagerly as if nothing had happened. He would say, "C'mon, Sandy, we're just going through a rocky time."

When I pleaded with Jeff to see a therapist, he still resisted.

"What good will that do?" he'd argue. Then another fight would ensue.

Sometimes, while we were arguing, Jeff would suddenly put his head in his hands in defeat. It was like a switch went off in his head. He would calm down, and the long-winded, sheepish apology would begin. Again, I felt like I was married to Dr. Jekyll.

It always seemed to crop up no matter how hard Jeff tried to hide his addiction. One night, I borrowed Jeff's car to run an errand. While I was out, I got a flat tire at the supermarket. I drove to a gas station where a teenage attendant offered to change the tire. He opened the trunk and unscrewed the top of the spare. Strategically placed around the tire were six beer cans. "Oh," I said, as my face grew red, "they're not mine—my husband must have put them there." The kid couldn't have cared less. I, however, was mortified. When I got home, I told Jeff.

"I'm sorry you had to be embarrassed in front of that kid," he said and left the room. I wanted to tear his head off.

Another time, Kevin needed a receipt, and I had to sort through the trash to find it. I found squashed-up beer cans wrapped in paper towels. "What is *this?*" I asked.

"They were the only beers I've had this week. I didn't want you to know I was drinking at all." Then he accused me of overreacting. I exaggerated and had "such an imagination."

"It's no big deal!" he would shout, turning into a raving maniac.

I'd have to bite my tongue. "If you won't stop drinking and hiding your booze from me, at least stop for the children!" I would plead. But I knew: Jeff couldn't stop drinking any more than he could stop breathing.

Later that week, Jeff drove Kelsey and me to her gymnastics dinner in his car. Several beer cans rolled out from under the seat when we stopped at a light. Kelsey was old enough to know what this meant. But she refused to acknowledge it. I could tell she was upset inside. Jeff sulked for the rest of the night. Clearly, he was disgusted with himself. On the other hand, Kelsey and I just wanted to forget about it and enjoy the night.

Later, I asked Jeff to clean up his car—at least when he knew Kelsey would be with us. Again, he shouted sarcastically, "If I can't drink in front of you, then I have to hide it." He always tried to blame me: if I would just let him drink, we wouldn't have a problem!

Jeff had a nervous habit of biting his fingernails. Around this time, I noticed him biting them more and more. He would bite them so hard that his cuticles would bleed. He developed other nervous habits too. He would pace through the first floor, mumbling to himself or no one.

Then he would bark orders at me or ask me random questions. The only thing consistent about Jeff's behavior was his inconsistency. Sometimes he would grab his keys and disappear in the car for hours at a time. When he returned, he seemed pensive and obsequious. "I'm so sorry for giving you such a hard time," he would say. "Please don't leave me. I can't live without you and the kids." I never knew which Jeff would appear: the belligerent one or the sheepish one.

Deep down inside, I knew I should leave the marriage, but I had convinced myself that I couldn't do it alone. I knew Jeff would make it difficult for me. Divorce would mean opening Pandora's box. I shuddered to think of what might fly out of it. How would we divide up the contents of our house after twenty-one years of marriage? Who would take the TV? What would we do with the photos of the kids? Who would get the computer? It was all too much to fathom. Besides that, I didn't have a regular paycheck. How would I begin to support myself and the kids without a job? I kept telling myself things would get better—and strangely felt comfort in the fact that, at the very least, he wasn't having an affair!

But I was fooling myself. Jeff was deeply involved in a love affair—with alcohol. That glistening, curvy bottle was his nightly seductress. She was always ready for him and would happily fulfill his deep, insatiable desires at a moment's notice. All he had to do was open his mouth and pour her down his throat. Within moments, she would ooze through his veins, numbing his pain and providing hours of delicious ecstasy. Jeff couldn't stop himself. He wanted to, but by now, he was so deep in this affair that there was no turning back.

Jeff couldn't let things slide off his back either with his anger and disappointments. Other memories floated back from the rear mental shelf where they had been pushed. Jeff secretly was haunted and terrified as they came back. It was way too painful and required more courage and diligence than he had. If he was never released from the enslavement of those dire secrets, he might never find sobriety.

He began to remember long-suppressed traumatic events from the past that were emotionally devastating to relive. Suddenly, explosive feelings erupted that he had not been capable of handling at the time of the trauma. They were uncontrollable and terrifying, and he probably feared they would never stop. This emotional trauma was as disturbing as the physical. It was crucial to take time to heal and recover from the effects of past abuse, abandonment, and violation. He didn't have a choice as a child and had had to remain in a potentially violent situation.

In April 2005, Jeff had been with his company for seven years—a monumental feat considering his drunken, erratic behavior at home. A friend often commented, "He must be very good at what he does to hold down a job." I was surprised when he came home from work one day with news that he had been chosen for a distinguished service award. To honor him, his company would host a banquet at a lovely restaurant in Jersey City overlooking Lower Manhattan.

The weekend included a stay at a luxury hotel and tickets to a Broadway show of our choice. I was thrilled. It would be the first time we had had a romantic weekend getaway. Maybe this was just what Jeff and I needed to get our marriage back on track. More importantly, I thought, he's finally getting the recognition he deserves. Maybe this would give Jeff a much-needed boost of confidence. Jeff came home from work early on the day of the banquet so we could get a head start on our weekend. We loaded up the car, kissed the kids goodbye (they were staying with friends), and arrived at the hotel just in time for happy hour. Jeff, of course, was only too happy to oblige. At dinner, wine, champagne, and mixed drinks flowed. Jeff was in his element, telling jokes and captivating his coworkers with his wry sense of humor. I remember beaming with joy watching Jeff work the room. This was the happy, gregarious, well-respected man I once knew. He was indeed the successful businessman I had imagined him to be. I was never prouder of him.

Jeff graciously accepted his award at the podium. Still, he suddenly became dark and cynical when he stumbled back to his seat. He muttered something about the company president being two-faced. His speech was slurred, his eyes vacant. It was midnight, and I knew it was time to get him back to the hotel. Jeff quickly passed out on the bed with all of his clothes on. Soon enough, though, he was up, pacing the floor and complaining loudly about his severe stomach pain. He proceeded to throw up all night long. "Must have been that Chateau Briand," he said.

The next morning, we scrapped our plans to go to *Phantom of the Opera* in New York. I was livid. I grabbed the keys from Jeff's hand and threw the suitcase in the back of the car. We drove home in silence. I thought about how Jeff had sabotaged this wonderful opportunity for us to celebrate his success. I knew from my Al-Anon meetings that self-loathing and contempt are typical of an alcoholic, but pitiful as it seemed; I couldn't help but feel hatred for him at that moment. I glanced at him from the corner of my eye. He looked relaxed and completely satisfied, almost smug, with the outcome of last night's drunken masquerade. Nobody knew his dirty little secret. What a feeling of victory he must have felt at that moment as we sped towards the ever-deepening black hole in front of us.

Jeff didn't talk about the banquet for the rest of the weekend. But he did remind me several times about the bad meat he had eaten.

If anything was unpleasant, I refused to believe it existed, and everything was "fine." So, peace didn't reign in our house. We yelled, and after a terrible, emotionally exhausting night of arguments, blame, promises, threats, and fear, Jeff would leave for work, kissing me on the way out the door. He often said, "Don't worry, everything is fine now. I love you, and I'll see you later."

And so, it was...until I started obsessing over what to do. Denial was a pattern of a lifetime for me also, and I practiced it without question for years. I began to search where I knew he had hidden his supply. I waited until he entered the bathroom to grab his key, run out to his car, and pop the trunk, expecting to find his stash. I didn't always gloat when I unearthed some evidence that only proved I was right. And I was disappointed when there was nothing tangible to back up my suspicions. I would then agonize over when and how I would confront him with my findings. I knew all hell would break loose. How dare I accuse him of drinking when I had no evidence. Often, I would choose to say nothing and ignore it so we wouldn't argue again. I wanted peace at all costs. Or I ranted and raved, and he promised it would stop or said I was crazy to make such a big deal out of it.

Jeff experienced blackouts, periods when everything he said and did vanish from his memory. After a night of outrageous drunken behavior, it was hard for me to believe that he couldn't recall his appalling actions that were so indelibly etched in my mind. I accused him of lying.

He stormed out of the room as a raving maniac. There was a commotion in the kitchen as he grabbed another beer from the back of the refrigerator. He reappeared in the doorway.

"Well, what have you decided?" he asked.

He looked pitiful, and I got hysterical when he provoked me again. I despised him for being unable to control his desire to drink, and I hated myself for reacting to him. Usually, when he was acting erratically, I tried not to antagonize him. I just walked away. I thought he was simply irresponsible, inconsiderate, and lacking in common sense. A sob caught in my throat, and I quickly turned away. Although he tried to act nonchalant, he was visibly frightened. Perhaps he sensed my resolve to leave him. He announced that he needed help and called AA.

He eavesdropped on my phone calls. I confronted him; he denied it. He was irritable, muddled, self-absorbed, unreliable, and unavailable when sober.

I lay in bed nauseated at night, listening to the footsteps going into the basement or the garage door slamming. I heard the tab on the can pop and the gurgle of fluid passing down Jeff's throat. I heard him sigh with contentment.

Eventually, Jeff's co-workers began to catch on to his behavior. When I was heading into a restaurant to celebrate my fiftieth birthday with my girlfriends, he called me in a panic because someone had complained to his boss that he smelled like he'd been drinking at work. "Well, were you?" I asked. He got mad at me for not siding with him and hung up. Then he called back, apologized, and told me it must have been the couple of beers he had had the night before. "I must still smell," he said sheepishly.

There was nothing I could do or say that would help Jeff. "Figure it out on your own," I told him. My tolerance for his self-pity was at an all-time low. Yet again, he had almost succeeded in tormenting me from afar, and this time I wasn't going to listen.

Soon enough, the company gave Jeff an ultimatum: go into rehabilitation or lose his job. Jeff chose rehab. This was a major turning point. I felt hopeful that this would be the incentive he needed to turn his life around. However, Jeff used it as an opportunity to feel remorse for himself again. "I wouldn't wish this problem on anyone," he said glumly. "I never wanted to become like my mother. I never meant for my life to end up this way."

Meanwhile, being the enabler, I took it upon myself to make dozens of phone calls to get Jeff into a program as soon as possible. I was able to get him an appointment with a substance abuse counselor early the next morning. And Jeff, true to form, drank before the appointment. The counselor made Jeff take a breathalyzer test, which proved he was already drunk.

Finally, the drinking took its toll, and Jeff checked into Sunrise House, an inpatient facility. "Your husband is very ill and in deep denial," the counselor told me. I felt emancipated because someone had finally confirmed what I had known.

It was a relief to finally have Jeff in the hospital and out of my hair. He, however, was miserable. He blamed everyone for his drinking problem. He refused to admit he *had* a problem. He was not allowed to place or receive any phone calls. Somehow, however, Jeff managed to call home after three days.

When I picked him up at the end of the week, he did nothing but complain. "That place did nothing to help me," he said. He never wanted to go back.

"I'm not like the rest of those guys. They are really bad with their problems," he claimed. "I'm not an alcoholic or drug addict like they are."

I signed an agreement that said if he drank again after the week in treatment, I would leave the marriage.

I was thrilled, relieved, and convinced everything would be fine now. He completed the week and seemed devoted to recovery for a very short while. Time passed. Then the drinking began again. I was stunned. I scolded, wept, threatened, fantasized, and demanded that he change.

I felt lonely, abandoned, angry, frustrated, and totally out of control. I thought I was going crazy. I was in the throes of his active, unarrested alcoholism. I was full of self-recriminations—for "failing" to make the marriage work, for being smart, independent, cold, caretaking, and everything else I was and wasn't. The next action plan was to get Jeff outpatient counseling and have him attend AA meetings daily. Later, he told me that he would first stop at a liquor store on the way to a meeting, drink a couple of beers in the parking lot, and then go inside. He said he did this because he was nervous. He would sit in the back of the room and refuse to participate. Clearly, he wasn't ready to admit he had an addiction. Jeff was destined for failure if he couldn't find a reason for being there.

During group sessions, Jeff didn't feel like he belonged. He couldn't admit to any weaknesses or bare his soul in front of anyone, let alone a group of strange men. He felt intimidated and wanted out. He preferred to talk to a private therapist. The substance abuse counselor encouraged Jeff to stay.

He looked him right in the eye and said, "You can do all the therapy in the world for years. Your problem is with alcohol addiction, and you need to face that." Jeff was unmoved. "You will lose jobs, and Sandy will take the kids and leave you," the counselor continued. "You have a serious problem and need to address this now and in this way!" But Jeff continued to resist. He dared to believe that he was in control of his addiction.

I believed the counselor. He was a decent man who was a recovering alcoholic himself. He saw people like Jeff all the time. He knew his kind. He gave Jeff the facts about what would likely happen down the road if he didn't admit his addiction. Jeff blew him off and decided to keep doing things his way. On the upside, Jeff began to see a sympathetic private therapist who quickly earned Jeff's trust. He was able to get Jeff to discuss his painful childhood. Somehow, Jeff let his guard down enough so the therapist could tap into the raw memories that had plagued Jeff all of his life. Jeff was opening up, which was a real breakthrough. I was excited to see the positive changes. Again, I was hopeful; things were looking up.

Unfortunately, the therapist could only get so far with Jeff, who cleverly concealed his addiction. Later, when Jeff returned to work, he purposely claimed he was too busy to get to his therapy appointments and quit. He did manage to keep up with his AA meetings. Still, He continued to adamantly refuse to work the program—although he admitted drinking in the parking lot before attending many meetings!

I heard myself remark, even so casually, "Where is your meeting tonight?" (Translation: "You *are* going, *aren't you?*")

Amazingly, the family had survived a relatively intact crisis for the first time. But the next time, everything fell apart. He sounded unmoved if I asked him how it felt to be sober. "I feel OK not drinking," he answered passively. Jeff resented his questioning at work when the boss asked how he was doing. He saw it as an interrogation. He was unhappy and wanted to change positions within the company. Soon after, in September of 2005, he was laid off again. Jeff was relieved. I was devastated.

Love

Chapter 12: Echoes of the Past

At this point, I stopped asking *why* and started asking *how*. How did our love come to this? How much longer could I take being in this loveless, abusive marriage? Often, Jeff cornered me, testing my resolve. I would roll my eyes. "Stop doing this," I said to him confidently. "You have a problem. You are an alcoholic."

With clenched fists, he said, "It's not that bad."

Sometimes I was immobilized, unable to do anything other than think about Jeff and his actions. His behavior became my sole focus. This was not love; it was an obsession. I ceased to live my own life because I was so preoccupied with him, and my behavior was almost always motivated by fear. It was harmful to our marriage for me to hover anxiously or suspiciously over Jeff, but it was also extremely self-destructive.

When Jeff's harsh words, groundless insults, outrageous lies, changes of plan, or unacceptable behavior came my way, I took it personally. When it didn't work, I would be proven right and feel smug. I continued in this self-righteous, martyr-like fashion, imagining myself fixing this "thing." "Not now," I snapped, walking away when he wanted to rehash some tiny detail to make himself feel better. "I don't have time to figure you out right now!" I'd spit out. I was surrounded by crisis, chaos, fear, and pain: turmoil. He claimed that his breath smelled from mouthwash or even hand sanitizer that he had rubbed on his face. Inside me, something snapped. *How stupid do you think I am?*

Blaming others for the consequences of his choices and acting out verbally were some of the smokescreens that Jeff used to conceal the real source of trouble—alcoholism. My attention went to the harsh word, the damaged car, and the loss of a job rather than this disease.

It was automatic to defend against the insult, cry at the additional expense of repairing the bumper again, and scramble to help him work again. But by naming the disease, I wasn't any longer distracted by it. I often detached with resentment, bitter silences, and loud and angry condescension. I coldly distanced myself with walls instead of necessary boundaries.

During the fall of 2005, Jeff was becoming manic. He couldn't sit still. He was constantly on the move, driving back and forth between our house in Chatham and the house at the shore. Desperate to find a job, he searched the Internet, called old colleagues, and sent out resumes. He only stayed in one place long enough to sleep—then he was back on the road again, running from his demons. The best part for me was when he took off to go down to the Jersey Shore and spent a couple of days away. I absolutely lived for these breaks from his insanity. I got a full-time job as a pet sitter, which gave me a newfound sense of independence—and the ability to plan and save money for my departure from the marriage. Each day I left the house with a smile on my face, knowing I was one day closer to leaving Jeff. Because of my schedule, I was in and out of the house all day. I never knew which Jeff I'd find when I returned home—or if I'd find him. It could have been Jeff, the Belligerent, Jeff the Complainer, Jeff the Moody, or Jeff the Meek. No matter which Jeff it was, our nights always ended with the two of us fighting.

Nothing I said or did was right at this point. He was so beside himself with anger toward me for even thinking about leaving him. I was once his entire support system, his sounding board, and had tolerated his mood swings. I always translated negativity into a positive glass half full. He got angry when I didn't say the right thing. I repeated, "Since I'm not saying exactly what you want me to say, why don't you write it down so I can read it! That way, I can get it perfect and not screw it up, and you'll shut up!"

I tried to keep our arguments to a minimum in front of Kelsey (by now, Kevin was a sophomore in college), but invariably, she would hear us. Sometimes she would run into her room and slam her door. Other times, she would cry and beg us to stop. Jeff liked to antagonize me in front of her just because he knew I would have to stifle my reaction to spare her from another fight.

As I became more independent, Jeff became more afraid of me. I was gaining the upper hand in our relationship, which made him angry. He knew I was preparing to leave him. Yet I was bewildered at his desperate, changeable state of mind. In one breath, he would beg me to stay. "Just stay until I get another job," he cried. "Please, I love you and can't live without you!"

I, however, didn't care anymore. Nothing he said or did would lessen my resolve. So, I simply ignored him. Then he would try a different, pity-seeking tactic. "You're wrong and crazy to stay with me," he'd say. "I have too many problems!"

It took an immense effort and commitment to stay with Jeff. It was eating me alive. I was nervous and tense. Drama, fear, secrecy, and hopelessness permeated our lives during his relapses. It was so overwhelming that the kids and I barely existed. I was preoccupied with trying to find a solution by persuading, coercing, begging, negotiating, and bribing. It was ridiculous. Being kind and understanding meant I said nothing, tolerated the intolerable, and suffered silently. For years, I denied the impact of living with an alcoholic husband.

There were so many times in his drinking career that we both thought all he had to do was control the amount and stop after a certain number. Unfortunately, the first drink began the merry-go-round. We talked endlessly about how to figure this out, playing Russian roulette with his health and mental and spiritual being. I was bewildered by the mysteries of his behavior. I didn't comprehend the abusive tirades and accusations since there was always an apology the next moment or day. We were locked in our positions and incapable of calling a truce most of the time. He was furious at me for challenging him. We were doomed as our marriage disintegrated and Jeff's addiction exploded. I dreaded every conversation.

Months passed, and Jeff was still unable to find a job. His moods grew worse. Each day, the mailbox was full of rejection letters, making Jeff hate himself even more. He refrained from drinking when he went on interviews but picked up right where he left off as soon as he got home. Jeff, the "dry drunk," was just as critical, confrontational, and overpowering as Jeff, the full-blown drunk. He became more distant and removed each week, and he still had not found work.

In the spring of 2006, Jeff finally got a job in the human resources department of Sunguard Trading and Risk Management Company. He had been out of work for nine months. His spirits lifted, but his outlook on our marriage remained dim. "Don't worry; I'll be out of here right after getting this job." He promised.

I wanted to believe that he was done being married too and would soon move out. Could it be that I would soon be free of Jeff? Or would this be yet another one of Jeff's empty promises?

The company Jeff worked for had two locations: one in Jersey City and one in Parsippany. Jeff commuted between both places and quickly calculated where each liquor store was along the way. He would stop by these landmarks to get his fix of beer or wine before, during, and after work. Then, alone in empty parking lots, he would fill himself up with his numbing nectar.

One day that summer, shortly after Jeff was hired, I was on the phone with a girlfriend when the call waiting signal beeped. I saw that it was Jeff. "Get off the phone," he said frantically. "I have a problem at work."

I started shaking. I knew that whatever it was had to do with Jeff's drinking. "What's wrong now?" I screamed, "Are you drinking on the job again?"

Jeff told me his coworkers had complained that he smelled like a drunk. "They're watching me," he said. A week later, he was fired.

I couldn't even look at him when he came home that Thursday after Labor Day to tell me he had lost his job. Inside me, something snapped. I said one more time, very calmly, "I can't live like this anymore. I want a divorce."

He explained how his employer had given him the option of going into rehab or facing termination. He chose not to go back to rehab. Hence, he was fired. Once again, he refused to admit he had a problem. It was *their* fault, not his.

He decided he was going to the shore for a few days to have time to think things over and lick his wounds. I knew this was just an excuse to go off on another bender. There was nothing I could do to stop him; frankly, I was quite relieved that he was leaving. "Just be out of here when I get back," I screamed as I headed out the door—ironically, to an Al-Anon meeting. It took an immense effort and commitment to stay with Jeff. It was eating me alive. I was nervous and tense and denied the depth of the alcohol problem.

Secrecy enveloped our home. Drama, fear, and hopelessness permeated every room during Jeff's relapses. The reality of our circumstances was overwhelming. Our lives were so wound up in Jeff's daily concerns that the kids and I barely existed. We were preoccupied with finding solutions to his drinking by persuading, coercing, begging, negotiating, and bribing. It was ridiculous because only Jeff knew the extent of his alcohol abuse: how much and where he drank and hid his liquor. Being kind and understanding meant I said nothing, tolerated the intolerable, and suffered silently. For years, I denied the impact of living with an alcoholic husband. An optimistic person by nature, I became hopeless.

I had become less tolerant and began to cling less pathetically to the marriage. I didn't panic at the possibility of upsetting the equilibrium of our family. As icy clarity seeped in, I realized with horror that I was repeating history. I came to believe that I needed to leave him.

My words spewed out—judgmental, negative, defeatist. I intended to be kind and tolerant, but some uncontrollable impulse to scream at him hit me. Jeff seemed diminished; his apology half-hearted. I no longer cared. I was tired of investing so much time and energy. The tearful good-byes were still far off, but I had resigned myself to nothing changing if I stayed married. I was hungover with tension after every relentless surge of adrenaline. I wanted to sleep with the exhaustion of being a peacemaker and rescuer. The next day, I picked up the phone and called another divorce lawyer. I was now more determined than ever to end my marriage. I really didn't care what happened anymore.

I needed out. I wasn't a monster because I wanted a divorce. I constantly prayed that Jeff would find sobriety. I sympathized with his job losses, disease, and lousy childhood. There was no malicious intent with my actions, only an incentive to get away from him. I couldn't stay out of obligation or pity or even for the children. I turned my attention to my lifetime of denial and finally began divorce proceedings. I began to act decisively, being cautious but defensive. The clarity didn't happen overnight, but I eventually decided that I absolutely, unequivocally was not going to remain married to Jeff.

His face grew dark. "How could you leave me?" he seethed. "Do you realize what this will do to the kids?" I was so afraid he would attack me. And when he came toward me in a rage, I ran up the stairs two at a time to get away, thinking I could safely barricade myself in my room. He was right behind me, licking at my heels as I raced up the stairs. He cursed me out, then shut the door and cornered me in the bedroom.

"Leave me alone; I want to get out. I have every right to get a divorce and every reason. You've had plenty of chances to clean up your act! Now I am finished trying." He laughed and said, "Good luck; it's not going to be that easy!"

I lost my patience and grabbed his hand to try to escape the room. My fingernail caught his skin, and he started to bleed slightly.

He screamed at me. "Now look what you've done; you are hitting me now?" I barked, "No, I'm just trying to get away from you; let me out of the room now!"

I was like a cornered animal, and he knew it. At that moment, I knew that nothing would change my mind about leaving my abusive, alcoholic husband.

Jeff was living at the shore full time, and I was living in Chatham with Kelsey. Every day we were apart, I felt stronger and happier and knew I would never return to the marriage. I felt sorry for him; I may have even still loved him, but my sanity depended on my staying away from his insanity. I was propelled into beginning a new future for myself. I was no longer trapped and inundated with Jeff's presence.

I got some perspective on my life. Alcoholism wasn't dominating every conversation. I knew I would be better off without being married to him, and I was so free. During the separation, neither child ever questioned my decision to leave. They witnessed the consequences of our dysfunctional marriage and Jeff's spiraling disease. They understood that I had to leave for my own sanity. I changed all the banking information, got new credit cards in my name, paid all the bills, and with my new pet-sitting job, I had enough income to support Kelsey (with Kevin away at college). I was managing, even thriving, despite the logistics of trying to unravel my twenty-three-year marriage with Jeff.

During the fall of 2006, Jeff lived at the shore house while he desperately (yet again) tried to find another job. He would return to Chatham every Saturday to visit Kelsey and treat her to lunch, the mall, or horseback riding, then drive back down to the shore that evening and return Sunday again to see her. This was a perfect setup for me. I had my independence back, Jeff left me alone, and he still spent time with Kelsey. We were on our best behavior, too. We were actually cordial with each other on the phone and in person. Sometimes I would buy him extra house supplies and food to return to the shore. It was beginning to look like we could work out this new arrangement of living apart.

Then, a week before Thanksgiving, Jeff dropped a bomb. On one of his Saturday afternoon visits, he announced, "I'm moving back here next Saturday!" My jaw dropped. I thought about what my lawyer had told me to do if he tried to move back in. "Oh, no, you're not!" I said. "You live at the shore now, and you can't just come back when you want to!"

"Oh, yes, I can, and I will!" he shouted back. "This is *not* your house. I can come back anytime I want!"

And Jeff showed up the following Saturday with all his possessions and began to move in. And as quickly as he came in the door with armloads of boxes, I worked just as fast, frantically carrying everything back out to the car. I was crying and shouting through my tears. "You can't do this!" I told him. "I'm divorcing you, and I can't live with you anymore!"

Later that afternoon, he finally left for dinner with Kelsey. To my surprise, my girlfriend suddenly showed up, who had encouraged me for years to leave Jeff. She had been thinking about me and was back east for a visit from her home in Colorado. As my guardian angel, she knew intuitively that I needed her there at that moment. She convinced me I needed to act immediately to get a restraining order against Jeff to prevent him from moving back in.

My girlfriend drove to the police station while my body trembled as I thought about the confrontation ahead. The police were understanding, but since there was never any physical violence, the judge couldn't grant the order over the phone. The officers tried to reach Jeff on his cell, but he clearly avoided their calls. They escorted me back to the house so they might talk to him, but he wasn't home. Soon after they left, he returned. "What have you done?" he asked me incredulously. "What did you tell them?"

"I told them we were separated and that you don't live here anymore." "Do you already have a boyfriend?" he shot back.

"No, of course not!" I answered defensively.

"Why can't we try and work on the marriage?" He was desperate now. "I still want to get back together."

But I was spent. The damage was done; I wasn't backing down. "Get out now, Jeff," I said firmly. Jeff left the room, gathered a few belongings, and walked out the door.

I had scored my first victory. I felt as though I was finally making myself clear. After years of being wishy-washy with Jeff, I felt bold and empowered standing up to him.

When the judge and police suggested I apply for the restraining order in person at the courthouse the following Monday, I didn't bother. Had I pursued it, the judge would have granted me one, considering that Jeff had a history of severe alcoholism. The cops and the judge asked me if I had filed for divorce yet, so I clearly needed to take the next step.

So instead of pursuing the restraining order, I called my lawyer and set up an appointment for that afternoon to file papers for divorce. I had never felt so empowered before in my life. There was no turning back now.

Right after I filed, my lawyer advised me to change the locks on the doors, which I did right away. I never told Jeff, so when he tried to open the door with his key, and it didn't work, he became livid. He called me at work and insisted I get home immediately to let him in. He threatened to break a window. If I didn't get home right away, he said, he would call the police and tell them I had locked him out of his own home.

I was so scared that I called the police and explained the situation. Shortly after, I came home to find two police cars in front of the house. Jeff had had the advantage of telling the police his side of the story first, and I could tell they must have thought I was a crazy, vindictive wife who was out to destroy her husband. When I went inside and told the officers about Jeff's erratic past, his harassment, and his drinking, they looked at me with a more sympathetic eye. I explained that I had filed for divorce, that we were living apart, and that my lawyer had advised me to change the locks. In the end, the police convinced Jeff to return to the shore and leave me alone. I did not know it then, but Kelsey had been upstairs listening to the entire exchange. She was understandably upset. Naturally, Jeff blamed me for causing it.

Despite being locked out and the reprimand from the police, though, Jeff tried to move back in several more times. He was like a dog scratching at the door. He claimed that I had kicked him out when he was fired from his job. He simply wanted to be back in our lives again. He couldn't understand why I wanted out, even though most of our marriage had been contentious. Oddly, he kept referring to our house as "the marital home" and that he had a "right" to move back in. I wondered if this wasn't his lawyer's advice. But through Jeff's distorted prism, he felt that we were just taking a break and honestly thought we would get back together.

Jeff's father had a stroke around this time. Pop was in the hospital and physical rehabilitation in Morristown for several weeks. Jeff used this as an excuse to drive from the shore every day to see Kelsey *and* visit his father. There was nothing I could do to stop him; after all, I still wanted him to have a relationship with Kelsey. He called incessantly to check on my whereabouts, sometimes from the highway or driveway. He demanded that I let him in to use the house phone, the computer, and the television.

Invariably, he would launch into his daily verbal assault: "Do you really hate me that much, Sandy?" or, when he was full of self-pity, "I can't help it if I can't stop drinking; I have a disease."

I was always careful with my words. "I'm not trying to harm you, Jeff," I'd say. "Let's just do this quickly and amicably." And, "You can't talk me out of it!" He needed a different explanation every day for why I wanted a divorce.

I tried to stay two steps ahead of Jeff, always trying to anticipate his next move. But this was virtually impossible, considering his erratic, alcoholic behavior. Changing the locks on the doors seemed to bring him to a new level of anger. He wanted revenge. He called me shortly after the lockout incident and surprised me. "This is a courtesy call," he said snidely. "I just canceled the joint Visa card, so you can't use it anymore."

Luckily, I had anticipated this and already had a new account in my name. I couldn't begin to imagine all the other things he was doing that he *didn't* tell me about.

Jeff's visits became more frequent. Sometimes he knocked on the door several times a day. He called the house or my cell phone, constantly checking where or who I was with. When I finally caved in and picked up the phone, he wanted to know why I hadn't answered it. Then he would slam the phone down and say he didn't want to talk to me anyway. He would do the same thing to Kelsey. This was Jeff's sick way of reaching out to both of us so that we would take him back in. His temper became worse than ever.

I dreaded every conversation but tried to placate him, being polite and helpful. I didn't know what to expect minute to minute. He deliberately agitated and tormented me with a million tiny questions just to interact with me.

Slowly but surely, Jeff lost the power of choice. His fears of failure were relentless. He was remorseful and filled with despair, confusion, frustration, and anxiety. Around the Christmas holidays, he had started to frequent bars and was drinking heavily. This was a dangerous combination. He was an angry, lonely alcoholic around a bottomless supply of liquor. Sometimes, when he came to the door, he was arrogant and defiant, demanding that I let him in. Sometimes, he'd be meek and remorseful, apologizing for everything he had done.

When I returned from being out, his car would often be in the driveway. Once, he sat in his car down the street and watched for my return, then appeared right behind me as I walked in the front door. If my car was parked in the driveway, he often parked his car right behind mine and honked loudly. This way, I couldn't leave. He'd box me in and make me beg him to move his car. He'd say he wanted to establish his right to be in "the marital home." He'd ask for another chance. He'd beg me to tell him what he did to make me want to divorce him. If I threatened to call the police, he'd tell me to go right ahead, this was his house too, and he could come in any time he wanted. Once, he said, "You better enjoy it while you can because it's not going to be yours for long!" But no matter what transpired, he would always leave in silence.

Around this time, I started to see a therapist to help sort out my future. She asked me what I was most afraid of while divorcing Jeff. She wanted to know if I thought Jeff was capable of hurting himself or me. I said no, he'd never do that. He wasn't that crazy. She wanted to know why Jeff was trying to make my life miserable and why he resisted me at every turn. I explained to her that it was impossible to deal with Jeff amicably when it was his alcoholism, not he, calling the shots.

By February 2007, Jeff had been out of work again for almost six months. He was drinking heavily, and his behavior was becoming increasingly erratic. He would call me in a rage and accuse me of being a terrible person for wanting a divorce and taking away his child. He'd blame me for all of his problems. I begged him to get professional help.

The night before I left to go to Florida with Kelsey for her school vacation, I was awakened by my cell phone ringing at 3:00 a.m. It was Jeff once again. He insisted that I leave the house unlocked when I left. He couldn't understand why I wanted to lock the doors and stop the mail while I was away for a few days! He threatened to break into the house if I didn't leave a key for him. "I want to be able to go into that house while you are away!" he shouted. I would never leave him a key, I told him several times before finally hanging up in tears. Not wanting to face another episode with the local police, I left the house unlocked just to keep him quiet. It wasn't worth arguing over anymore. I was so worn out from the bickering I no longer cared whether he came in while I was gone or not.

The entire four days we were in Florida, he called to torment me with questions about why I told my divorce lawyer to do this. He called on Kelsey's phone and insisted on speaking to me, then asked why he could only see Kelsey once a week. He said he would see her any day of the week he wanted.

The night before we were to fly home, Jeff called and insisted on picking us up so he could see Kelsey. But I had already arranged weeks to have a friend drive us home from the airport. I refused to ride in the car with him. I told him he could see Kelsey when we got home; we would take care of getting home ourselves. He then proceeded to call me a liar and a terrible, rotten person who wanted to take his child away from him. I couldn't escape his tirades, even when I was fifteen hundred miles away. Ironically, his car broke down, and he could not even meet us at the house. It was a good thing we weren't counting on him.

Once, during a snowstorm in February, Jeff attempted to drive up from the shore and spent four hours on the parkway before turning around. He called twelve times that day to say he couldn't get there. Another time he called on his way up, insisting that I had the electric bill ready for him when he came. When I told him no, he became belligerent. "Give me the fucking electric bill, or I'll break a window!" he screamed.

I dreaded his daily visits. I was more afraid of him than ever. I couldn't understand why he felt the need to drive up every day from the shore. It was both impractical and an imposition. If Kelsey was at a friend's house, Jeff insisted I call her to come back home. If she couldn't come home, he'd storm off in a huff and say, "You're keeping her away from me now, aren't you?" Even after Kelsey dropped everything to come home from her friend's house to see him, he would leave just as abruptly as he arrived, without as much as a goodbye. As soon as he walked out the door, I realized I had been holding my breath the whole time he was there.

At the beginning of March, Jeff demanded that I pay the yearly income taxes. He claimed that since I was working, I owed them money. I brought the tax forms and bank statements to my lawyer so he could examine them. He noticed a twenty-nine-thousand-dollar withdrawal from one of Jeff's retirement accounts. Jeff had cashed in one of his retirement funds in December, took a huge penalty, and now expected me to pay the large tax on it. When I asked Jeff about it, he said he didn't have any money and that it was my responsibility to pay the taxes on the early withdrawal. How could he not have any money? He was living rent-free at the shore house and still collecting unemployment for the second year in a row. He had had a checkbook with five thousand dollars in it when we separated and received two more paychecks after his termination in August. And now, what could he have done with another twenty-nine thousand?

Chapter 13: Relentless

Jeff had lost the power of choice. His fears of failure were relentless, as were his hurtful actions towards me. Around the Christmas holidays, he frequently visited bars and drank heavily. He was arrogant and defiant, demanding I let him in the house. Or he was meek and remorseful, apologizing for everything he had done.

Often, I would return to his car in the driveway. Or he would watch from up the street, then pull right behind me. Or appear out of nowhere walking in the door after me. Often, when I pulled in, he parked right behind me and honked loudly. He'd box me in and make me beg to move his car. He taunted, "I just want to establish my right to be in the *marital home*." Then he would storm off, yelling, "You better enjoy it while you can because it's not going to be yours for long."

A therapist that I started seeing not too long after all this asked me, "What are you most afraid of? Do you think your husband is capable of harming himself or you? Why is he trying so hard to make your life miserable? Why is he resisting you at every turn?"

Her questions hit home. The impact of her words was too real, and I didn't know what to think about it. I thought about it for a while, weighing my thoughts and words. And then, I said, "It's the alcohol calling the shots. It's impossible to deal with Jeff amicably because of his addiction."

I planned a trip to Florida to see my sister in February with Kelsey. It was my time to relax and unwind; that's what holidays are supposed to be about. But alas, that was not the case. Not on Jeff's watch.

The phone rang at three in the morning. It was Jeff.

The first thing he asked when I picked up the phone was, "Why are you locking the house? I need to be able to go into that house while you're away for four days. Either leave me a key, or I'll break the door down."

I felt a lot of things. I was somewhat still shocked that he was keeping tabs on me. I was surprised that he knew I had been locking up the house. I was pissed off that he called me at such an hour to remind me that I shouldn't be locking the door. He didn't even feel bad about it. I was furious that he felt so entitled and simply didn't care about anything except himself. Of course, this was not the end of it. The entire trip, he tormented me with something or the other. He had questions, so many questions.

Why do you want a divorce? What did you tell your lawyer? Why can't I move back in, see Kelsey more, go back to the way it was?

The night before we were to fly home, he insisted on picking us up. I said, "We are all set. You can see Kelsey at home."

He then called me a liar, a terrible, rotten person who wanted to take his child away from him.

"Okay, pick us up," I complied.

"Never mind, I don't want to see you," He quickly said and hung up.

During a snowstorm, he sat in the parkway for seven hours, trying to get to me. He called twelve times, insisting I have the electric bill ready. He became belligerent when I said no.

I still remember what he said, "Give me the fucking electric bill, or I'll burn down the house."

I was holding my breath every second of every day. I knew he was mad at me, but this erratic, irrational, and psychotic behavior was even worse than I had imagined. He was controlling, and when confronted with that idea, he would deny it to my face.

Jeff demanded that I should pay the yearly income taxes. He had been out of work again for nine months and was spending money constantly. I took the tax forms to the lawyer. He noticed a twenty-nine thousand dollar withdrawal from one of Jeff's retirement accounts. He had cashed it back in December, took a huge penalty, and now expected me to pay the hefty tax on it.

When I questioned him, he said he had no money.

I was incredulous and said, "You're living rent-free, collecting unemployment for the second year in a row, had money before we separated, and have received two more paychecks after you lost that job. And you now spent twenty-nine thousand more?"

I paid the income tax on the retirement account. It was just easier than fighting with him. He knew the best way to hurt me was through money. I needed to placate him during every confrontation. It made me feel defenseless and inadequate, but I knew I would never go back to the marriage we had. I needed to put aside these appalling behaviors and keep moving forward.

Chapter 14: Years of Denial

On March 15, while driving in Morristown, Jeff had a minor fender bender and got his first D.U.I. He called me from his cell phone, but I could barely understand his garbled words. He said something about coming to bail him out of jail. I wanted to help him but didn't want to send the wrong message.

I was clueless about what to do, so I called my lawyer. He advised me not to pick Jeff up. So, I left him there to spend the night. Jeff called me several times that afternoon, begging me to come and get him out of jail. " Come bail me out. I don't want to spend the night in jail. Don't you care about me at all anymore? He pleaded. I hoped this would be a turning point for Jeff. Maybe he would finally feel like he had hit rock bottom and get some help.

Bailing him out of jail would only perpetuate his pain. Sobriety continued to elude my husband. I couldn't keep the recriminations out of my voice, so I decided to break my old pattern of finger-pointing and let him figure out what happened for himself.

The next day, Jeff was released; he called me from his cell phone as he drove back to the shore. I was astounded that he could be back on the road so soon. Jeff did nothing but complain about being stuck in traffic. He never mentioned a word about being locked up in jail. I could sense that Jeff had felt no remorse. He made no apologies or admitted that he even had a problem with alcohol.

He found another lawyer in Morristown for the D.U.I. He was scheduled to return for his court date (which he later avoided by rescheduling it repeatedly). Had anyone known about the seriousness of Jeff's alcoholism, they would have revoked his license right then and there. So, without a conviction, he continued to drink and drive. And there was nothing I could do to stop him.

I switched lawyers in April. I needed someone who specialized in difficult divorces. I went back to the woman I had seen fifteen years earlier for advice. I was afraid and needed an expert to deal with this. When I went in for the consultation, she immediately understood my predicament and wanted to help. Imagine, it took me another fifteen years to come back around. I hired her on the spot.

Jeff's lawyer told him, "I was out to get him because of this new, top-notch lawyer." This made him paranoid, thinking I had some ulterior motive for leaving him. He called me the devil and accused me of "ruining his life."

One of the first things we did was forbid Jeff from driving Kelsey anywhere. If he wanted to take her out in the car, I drove her while he followed behind. Then I would wait around while they ate or shopped and come back to drive her home. He hated this, and so did I. He'd tell me not to arrive a minute too soon because he wanted to be with Kelsey every possible minute. I resented that my day revolved around his erratic schedule and the vagaries of his nomadic life.

To make matters worse, he was snide and cynical, "Don't be late or a minute early. You made this worse than it has to be. It's your fault we are dealing with this."

During these challenging encounters, I was conflicted about dealing with Jeff. I wanted to have compassion for him, especially because it was clear that he was suffering, and his life seemed to be spiraling out of control. But he needed to take ownership of his actions. He had created this mess of a life and had done nothing consistently to help himself. How much sympathy and patience did I have left inside for him? I thought he would have to face his demons at some point. By that time, we'd be divorced, and I wouldn't have to be there to pick up the pieces for him. All I wanted to do was get through the divorce amicably. I thought that was reasonable enough. Maybe then we could all begin to heal.

I could feel the world starting to close in on Jeff. His addiction and blossoming psychosis slowly shut him off from our children and me. It was beating the life out of him. I was consumed by fear each day, knowing Jeff was like a ticking time bomb. He might kill someone in a drunk-driving accident. His body might begin to shut down. I knew he could not go on living like this. The worse part is he didn't seem to care about anyone or anything anymore. This scared me more than his angry outbursts and irrational demands. Our relationship was tainted with doubt. I didn't trust he was doing what he said because he never kept his word. He lost credibility with Kevin and Kelsey, me, and himself. Every broken commitment had been a crack in the foundation of our life together, which would undermine his self-esteem.

Then, the guilt, shame, and betrayals acted as poison. Desolation and resignation set in as he realized the degree to which he had messed up. Ultimately, perpetuating our pasts damages the future. Jeff was incapable of forgetting one detail of his past misfortunes after they resurfaced. The awareness brought too much pain, and the drinking and depression episodes were more pronounced and frequent.

No matter how the arguments began, what they were about, or where they were going, I was beaten down until he just didn't care anymore. These battles were just a waste of time and energy. The passive-aggressive behavior left a rotten taste in my mouth every time. I adapted to these threatening situations by denying how horrible they really were. Leaving him required a lot of effort; I thought it would be a fiasco. After all, Jeff genuinely loved me, and maybe if I wished, prayed, and tried harder to please him, he would not get angry. This fantasy that I held on to kept me in this abusive marriage.

When I stared at my reflection in the mirror, I saw the hurt on my face and eyes. My share and guilt for not being able to fix our marriage were palpable, and the hopelessness was paralyzing. I wasn't equipped to move forward and let go of my loveless marriage, so I mentally erased the past pain. To acknowledge further victimization would have meant I needed to do something. I was preoccupied with keeping the drama at a minimum. I didn't comprehend the abusive tirades and accusations. I wanted and needed to believe what he was telling me.

I was bewildered by the mysteries of his behavior. There was always an apology in the next hour or the next day. We were locked in our positions and sometimes absolutely incapable of calling a truce. Our lives were being poisoned by his drinking and lying about it. He was furious at me for challenging him and at himself for being unable to stop. Jeff didn't respond well to disparagement; he usually became defensive and resistant. Men don't like being told what to do. One day without warning, he asked, "What did your lawyer send to my lawyer? I wasn't sure what he was referring to.

I said, "I'm not sure what you're talking about—visitation, the house, or what?"

He gruffly said, "Get the facts straight with your lawyer! How can you not know what was sent when telling your lawyer what to write to mine?" He was somewhat correct...I felt frozen, defenseless, frustrated, and indecisive, but I didn't always know exactly what was being documented. Frantically, I tried to give him the answer he wanted. It didn't matter what I said or did. He was mad, and I just wanted to get out of his way. I didn't know what to expect minute to minute.

Nothing I said or did was right at this point. He was so beside himself with anger towards me for leaving him. I was once his entire support system, his sounding board, and the person who tolerated his mood swings. I tried to translate negatives into positives, convincing him the glass was half full, not empty. He got angry when I didn't say the correct thing to him.

I repeated, "Since I'm not saying exactly what you want me to say, why don't you write it down so I can read it. That way, I can get it perfect and not screw it up, and you'll shut up for once!"

I wasn't a monster because I wanted a divorce. I constantly prayed during the marriage that Jeff would find sobriety. That was an illusion. He became very self-destructive and deteriorated drastically, even while we were together.

I sympathized and empathized with his job losses, disease, and lousy childhood; my actions had no malicious intent; I only had the incentive to get away from the marriage. It created a lifetime of falling for men who drank excessively and me subconsciously trying to fix them. I couldn't stay out of obligation or pity any longer, or even for the children. During the separation, neither child ever questioned my decision to leave. They witnessed the consequences of our dysfunctional marriage and Jeff's spiraling disease. They understood that I had to leave for my sanity.

Jeff had been hospitalized this one time. Yet, his physical compulsion and mental obsession to drink dominated his life. His willpower alone helped him through the years; it wasn't enough now. He would have benefited from more rehabilitation, more therapy, more faith, and more recovery.

Jeff had never deliberately wanted to cause so much trouble. He had experienced the inevitable consequences of irresponsible drinking growing up. Tearfully he said repeatedly, "I wouldn't wish this on anybody. I'm not a bad person. Why did this happen to me? Why can't I stop drinking? You're lucky; you dodged a bullet by not becoming like me."

My lawyer and I tried to negotiate an agreement allowing Jeff to parent Kelsey but protect her from harm. Jeff was to undergo a professional expert's alcohol evaluation on these issues. He was to submit to a breathalyzer test before six hours of parenting Kelsey. He had to forfeit that session with her if he didn't pass.

Jeff rarely saw his dad during our marriage except during a holiday dinner. Pop was evidently an abusive father and had dramatically impacted Jeff's sense of self-worth and self-esteem. He also hid behind the façade of having a father who was ill and dying, even though his relationship with his dad had been nonexistent for many years. He had not seen his dad for over a year before his father's stroke in December 2006.

During this time, my divorce lawyer had asked me to call daily to report Jeff's behavior and activity. I started documenting daily driving to the house in April, frantic phone calls, and rude hang-ups.

"I need to see the cover letter from the accountant. You call him and ask for an extension!" Jeff demanded.

I said, "You call him. I already called him last week. The returns have been sitting on the dining room table for weeks; you could have looked over them many times before now!"

He slammed the receiver down, then called back seconds later. "I'm coming up there today! Be there! And don't you dare lock the house on me, or I will call the cops!"

He called four times to talk to Kelsey about meeting for lunch. I found him walking in the door two seconds after me. Had he been waiting up the street? He headed back to the computer area. "Where are you going?" I inquired.

"I've got time to kill, so I'm going to check my e-mail."

"No, you can't come here to do that. Leave, or I'll call the police. You do not live here anymore, and you can't just waltz here and act as you do!"

"I'm not leaving until I want to! So just call the police, and I'll tell them it's still my house too!"

This mental torture continued for weeks. Jeff would call Kelsey several times in a few minutes to ask, "Do you want me to come to your lesson tomorrow?"

She said, "Come if you want!"

She didn't know what else to say or do. Jeff complained and whined that he didn't see her enough, but he came to the house every day to see her. Jeff's visits became more frequent. He would knock on the door several times a day. He constantly called the house or cell phone, checking where I was and with whom. When I answered, he would say he didn't want to talk to me anyhow and slam the receiver down again and again.

In May, Kelsey had gymnastics meet, and Jeff decided to drive up from the shore to see it. To her horror, he showed up drunk, yet again. After the competition, he approached her and wanted to take her out for lunch. But Kelsey wanted nothing to do with him. She wanted to go out with her friends instead. Why would she risk her life getting into a car with him when he reeked of alcohol? My heart sank as I saw her frightened expression, watching him sway and stumble back to his car that morning.

Though it was heartbreaking, Kelsey began to tire of being the sole focus of Jeff's life and his only joy and reason for existing. She had boundless compassion for him and loved him dearly. But she was also a 12-year-old teenager with a busy life, and her patience with his behavior was thin.

At the beginning of May, Kelsey was in a horse show. Jeff arrived late and wandered around the riding stable, waiting for Kelsey to perform. As she completed her competition, I watched Jeff walk to his car, open the trunk, and pull a can of beer from a large, black garbage bag. Then he got into the driver's seat, opened the beer, took a gulp, and drove away.

My lawyer had told me to call the police if I knew he was actively drinking and driving. I could have had him pulled over in an instant. Yet I was conflicted. Morally, I had an obligation to do the right thing, but I was afraid of what Jeff would do if he found out I had reported him. I am embarrassed to say I didn't call the police because it would irritate Jeff even more.

Chapter 15: The Beginning of the End

Towards the end of May, Jeff had started to leave cryptic messages on my cell phone, like "Tell the kids I love them because I won't see them again." Then he would call and tell me he wasn't a quitter, that he loved me, and that he would finally get some help. Soon after, he began sending me angry, ranting letters telling me how terrible a person I was and how much he hated me.

Jeff was slipping away. He was becoming manic. I begged him to get into rehabilitation - if anything for Kevin and Kelsey. He wouldn't come into the house to see Kelsey anymore. When he came to the door, his skin reeked of sweat and alcohol. He wasn't showering or shaving anymore. He was beginning to look like the skid-row bum people think alcoholics are.

In early June, he called to tell me he had made an appointment with a drug and alcohol counseling and rehabilitation facility in Summit. I was shocked but thrilled that he had finally taken the initiative to seek help. A week later, I learned that Jeff never went to that appointment. The multiple calls to Kelsey's cell, my cell, and the house phone tapered off. The continuous visits to the house stopped, except when he fell down the stairs with the filing cabinet. Kevin was getting frustrated and said, "Stay away until you go to rehabilitation."

Now he was demanding that I put mail in the mailbox. Suddenly he didn't want to come into the house anymore. Then he would be angry about the house again and wanted to go to Kelsey's gymnastic dinner. Two seconds later, he called and shouted, "You go, I'm too busy." My head was spinning. I was living in a nightmare-like scenario, and I couldn't wake up.

He came to the house unexpectedly. He looked very sick and complained of leg and back pain. I offered him a case of water, and as he popped the trunk, I saw a twenty-four pack of beer sitting there. He insisted on cutting the lawn and then complained the entire time.

I say, "You smell, don't drive."

The beer was gone from the car trunk, so he argued with me, "Mind your own business! Leave me alone. You're the problem."

I am being chased, trying to stay one step ahead of him but losing ground. Where did the case of beer go? Could he have drunk it already?"

He no longer insisted on coming into the house to see Kelsey. He continued to call and ask to use the Lavallette house. I was nervous about him driving on the parkway, but I said, "Yes, but please be careful.

Don't do anything crazy." Our entire lives were crazy already, but I said it anyway.

He talked some more about an appointment in Summit for counseling and rehabilitation. Again I was shocked but thrilled. I couldn't imagine what else would stop him from drinking himself to death. I've heard the phrase, "alcoholics have three choices: rehabilitation, jail, or death." I was sympathetic to his situation and pitied him as I watched him continue to spiral downward. I wanted him to rally and conquer all his problems, but I suspected he was beaten. I prayed for the best outcome every moment of every day.

Later that evening, Jeff called from the parkway. He asked, "Can I use the Lavallette house tonight? I want to go listen to a band in town."

I hesitated because I had planned on driving down the next morning. But I said, "Ok, but please leave before I get there. I don't want to have any problems or arguments.

I arrived at the house around 8:00 AM and knocked on the door since his car was still in the driveway. At first, Jeff refused to let me in. So I used my key and watched while he gathered up all his beer cans in the living room. Then he grabbed a large, black garbage bag and emptied the refrigerator. He looked horrible; it was obvious he hadn't slept all night. He was tormented by the D.U.I., divorce proceedings, childhood trauma, and mounting alcohol abuse. His life was descending into chaos as he tried to handle his addiction single-handedly.

I saw the resignation and agony in his eyes as he cried, "I don't know what to do anymore. I can't go on like this. You don't know what it's like to be sick like this. You just don't know how hard it is."

I said nothing. It was unbelievable how lost and beaten was this disheveled man who acted with so much desperation. Jeff was a bottomless well of restlessness, anxiety, and fear. His mind was no longer an ally, but a strangling, evil force that had malfunctioned with alcohol. He was overloaded with fear that was impossible to shut down; sleep was elusive. Jeff was consumed with self-doubt and alcohol-induced nausea. He desperately needed intervention but still couldn't admit to himself that there was a huge problem. He was embarrassed and humiliated by what had transpired over the last few months.

I watched Jeff stumble to the car with the black garbage bag filled with empty cans over his shoulder. He threw it in the back seat and drove down the street in eerie silence. My lawyer had repeated many times, "If you know he's intoxicated and driving, call the police so they can pick him up." I felt paralyzed with fear doing this.

As he drove away that morning, I was petrified he would get into an accident and hurt an innocent person. Jeff wouldn't have been able to submit or survive a stint in jail if this happened. And legally, I would have been held responsible also. That would have definitely been the last straw. I am thankful our children never had to visit Jeff in jail.

I spoke briefly to a neighbor that morning about Jeff. He said, "Your husband got a D.U.I. down here a short while ago." I nearly collapsed. I had no idea about this second offense. I called the police and asked, "Why didn't I know about this?" Why is he still driving? When did this happen?"

The officer explained, "Your husband was pulled over late at night Memorial Day weekend along the Bay Road for erratic driving. His blood alcohol level was two point eight. Had it been a three-zero, we would have transported him to the local hospital. He could barely stand up, repeat the alphabet, so we cuffed him and kept him overnight in jail."

I wondered again, "Why is he still driving? Wasn't his first D.U.I. from March 14th in the system?"

Apparently, since Jeff hadn't gone to court yet for the first offense, he could continue behind the wheel.

During this time, Jeff stopped by the house to see Kelsey less and less. Even the relentless phone calls tapered off. This was completely out of character and very troubling. I tried to relax and hope this meant Jeff was getting help, but I also thought he was just hiding.

A week or so later, Jeff informed us that he was scheduled for an interview with an alcohol rehabilitation center the following week. We had all waited for this moment when he would turn himself in and get the desperately needed help. Our divorce proceedings were at a standstill because he kept putting off treatment. This was a necessary step before we could agree to visitation, parenting, and the division of our assets.

But after a few days, Jeff called Kelsey and told her he loved her; he had decided not to go into rehab. "I have made other plans," he told her. She begged him to reconsider, "Dad, you have to do this now!" she pleaded. "Please go to that appointment and get yourself help. Did you read my letter? Please go get help today!"

That was the last communication we had with Jeff before he disappeared. He was M.I.A. over the next three weeks. He just dropped out of our lives. I kept expecting him to arrive at the house or call, but no word. I mentioned this to a friend, and she said, "Oh, he's probably just trying to fix his life. He'll be back, you'll see." This was not exactly comforting, but I tried to believe that he was in recovery somewhere in the middle of America. It was a relief not to be harassed and tormented by his irrational behavior. Our days were spent trying to pretend nothing was out of the ordinary. Kelsey and I spent some time away at the shore in Lavallette when I wasn't working in Chatham. Kevin would get away on weekends when he had some time off.

Chapter 16: The Ticking Time Bomb

On July 10, my neighbor and her daughter (Kelsey's good friend) came to the beach for the day. After a lovely day, we headed out to dinner when my cell phone rang. It was Kevin. He sounded panicked. He had just gotten off the phone with his father, who had been calling him repeatedly and threatening suicide.

I said, "Don't worry. I'll call him and tell him off the ledge. He's just crying wolf; he's bluffing. Call me back if he calls again." I honestly didn't think Jeff was capable of hurting himself.

Kevin did indeed call me back. I convinced him to go out with his friends and leave his dad with me. As I went to bed, I prayed Jeff would not follow his plan.

I was jolted awake by the house phone at 3:00 AM. It was the Morris County Park Police. Jeff had followed through on his threat. They found him bleeding in the woods of Loantaka Park.

"Sometime before dusk," the officer explained, "He had parked his car in the lot. When it was still there after dark, we became suspicious. We checked the license plates and called the house. Your son told us he threatened to hurt himself."

The police immediately began to search the woods for him. A short time later, they stumbled upon him deep in the woods, bleeding profusely and barely conscious. They told me he slit his neck, face, and wrists. He was in an ambulance on the way to Morristown Memorial Hospital.

"They will take care of him now." He assured me.

"There is nothing you can do tonight, so you might just as well go back to sleep."

I wanted to know if he was drunk. The officer said Jeff told him he'd had a few beers.

I said, "he's a raging alcoholic with two D.U.I.s already."

It didn't appear to faze the officers, who quickly ended the conversation.

I closed my eyes, but all I envisioned was the brutality of what Jeff had done. I thought of him lying in the darkness, drunk, alone, surrounded by poison ivy. I didn't know the severity of the wounds, but this was still a huge cry for help.

The next morning, I called Kevin. Jeff had left him a voicemail in the woods the night before. It said, "Kevin, help me. I cut myself, and now I need help." Kevin pointed out, "At least now we know where he is."

I called Susie, Jeff's sister. We hadn't spoken since last fall because of the divorce, but now we need to rally together. She had also been out of touch with her brother, so I filled her in.

"He's gotten two D.U.I.'s; his drinking has escalated, and nobody had seen or heard from him for three weeks until last night. He went into the park in Morristown and slit his face, neck, and wrists. The E.M.T.'s took him to the emergency room."

I also called the hospital, spoke with a social worker, and filled her in on some of the details of Jeff's life.

I repeated through the receiver, over and over, "My husband is a depressed alcoholic, and we are going through a divorce. His drinking has escalated, and I'm worried about his sanity." She sounded surprised I would describe him like this but was familiar with the addiction and cover-up.

She said, "Your husband is in total denial. He doesn't act drunk or out of control at all."

But no sane person cuts both his wrists like this, I thought.

Later that day, I had a similar conversation with another social worker and warned her that Jeff was very ill. Both realized I was not exaggerating when the delirium tremors and hallucinations began. They proceeded to treat Jeff's withdrawal accordingly. Also, from their experience, they judged Jeff as having a high risk of trying suicide again. This was not a "cry for help" but a serious effort to die.

My lawyer insisted I see a therapist who dealt with this kind of trauma. She also was the person who would evaluate Kelsey if I pushed for sole custody.

After I told her what Jeff did, she said, "There are alcoholics, and then there are people like your husband. This was a violent, cruel, bloody attempt at suicide. Putting it bluntly, it was a fuck that aimed toward you."

I was stunned. I was numb from the reality of what Jeff had done, and now I knew how much he hated me. At the same time, I felt enormous relief that he didn't die. We were all basking in the knowledge that he might find sobriety and hope for the future while in professional care. I relaxed a little, knowing where he was for the next couple of weeks.

Since I wasn't the contact person, I had little direct information after the first day. Jeff continued to try to control everything from the hospital bed.

He demanded, "Why can't Kevin be the contact person? I don't want Sandy to be that."

Susie was the most suitable since they had always had a wonderful, close relationship.

The following Sunday, Susie and her partner came from New York City to visit Jeff for the first time since he had tried to kill himself. Jeff had been moved from intensive care to the trauma surgery recovery unit. She kept me up to date, and we constantly talked about what to do, how to help, and what the future held for him.

They were visibly shaken up and told me, "He looked physically awful. He seemed severely depressed and very shaky. He was unstable and looked like he had just had a nervous breakdown." Susie continued, "He's heavily medicated for the pain and in shock. He's on a twenty-four-hour suicide watch; a man stood in the corner of the room during our visit. His arms are bandaged with splints up to his elbows to immobilize his damaged wrists."

She became emotional as she went on to say, "He had his wrists surgically repaired since he cut so deep down to the bone. The doctors hoped there would not be any nerve damage. He will need months of hand and wrist therapy to strengthen where he severed; even then, his wrists will be weak. When a bed is available, he will be moved to the psychiatric and behavioral health unit." I realized he had used the Cutco knife that is so sharp it cuts through metal. I also realized that Jeff could never live with this disability; the shame and horror of what he failed to accomplish would not let him be.

And he would undoubtedly try again.

Everyone was anxious about Jeff's mental condition and what the future held. I feared that with his fragile self-esteem, he might view this attempt at dying as one more failure. Also, now that he is sober for the first time in years. He had to face the reality of what he had done and deal with the devastation, but he couldn't drink to self-medicate.

Somewhere between the intensive care unit, the trauma surgery recovery unit, and the behavioral health unit, Jeff was prescribed antidepressant and antianxiety medications. A trained therapist assessed his situation and determined a treatment plan. He had a mental and emotional disorder in addition to alcohol abuse.

Of course, it would be impossible to figure out Jeff's entire psychological state in such a short time, but he showed signs of being profoundly disturbed. He needed years of treatment.

The social worker told Susie, "In group therapy at the hospital, Jeff wouldn't admit to attempting suicide." She indicated that in sessions, Jeff expressed that he was in the hospital because of an "accident" and would not discuss or admit to his alcoholism. This spoke volumes to the authorities about his denial and indicated his disturbed mental condition.

The following week, my brother and his girlfriend came for a visit from Minnesota. We were at the Lavallette house after a nice dinner when I got a voicemail from Jeff that said, "Meet me in front of Bamberger's with some clothes."

I was extremely confused and imagined him standing there for hours, waiting for me in his hospital gown with bandages on his arms. It didn't make sense that the hospital would release him in that condition. And Bambergers went out of business in 1986.

Moments later, my girlfriend called and said, "My husband wanted to go see Jeff tonight. When he spoke to the hospital front desk, they said Jeff had checked out." How could this be possible?

Kevin went to the hospital later to see whether he was there. Fortunately, he was. Kevin told me later, "Dad looked bad. I didn't know what to say."

The following Saturday, Susie and Sue saw Jeff in his behavioral health unit, also known as the "Franklin Five" or the "psych floor."

After their visit, we sat in the backyard. They reported, "Jeff looked and seemed better. He could hold a conversation and didn't act depressed or mentally unstable. He was far from being in a physical, emotional, or psychological state in which they could imagine him ready or even capable of living on his own again."

During this visit, Susie asked the front desk what the plan was for her brother. The attendant said, "Jeff will probably be discharged at the end of the week, around August 1. There are no plans for long-term inpatient care." Susie expressed grave concerns to the social worker about Jeff being released too soon.

The team member explained, "As long as he wasn't expressing any desire to try suicide again and wanted to get his life together, we can't keep him any longer, and insurance won't pay for it."

It was scary that he would be free to hurt himself again soon.

Soon after Susie and Sue got this information, they sent a letter to one of the doctors that had seen Jeff briefly. She described the dysfunctional household she and Jeff were raised in. Susie also mentioned the divorce, the job losses due to alcoholism, and his deterioration during the last couple of months. She explained," Jeff's self-esteem was virtually nonexistent and that he was extremely hard on himself. He refuses to work through the A.A. Program and refuses to see a doctor to regulate his depression and anxiety."

She wrote, "my brother needs long-term inpatient care. I honestly believe he will try again to end his life and succeed. Given the severity of the attempt on his life, he is considered high risk and a danger to himself."

Later that week, my brother, John, and Connie asked me, "would you mind if we went to see Jeff?" I thought this was a great idea. John is a recovering alcoholic, and Jeff often commented on how well he was doing.

When they entered the hospital room, Jeff seemed extremely agitated to see them. He ignored their questions if they mentioned the suicide attempt and changed the subject. They tried to get some idea about what he might want to do when he was released.

Jeff announced, "I have a plan.

There is more than one plan, but I'm not telling you what the plans are." They were afraid of what he was contemplating.

Jeff was scheduled to be in court in Lavallette during the hospital stay for the second D.U.I. He had not answered a couple of summons, and his New Jersey driving privilege would be suspended indefinitely. The social worker wrote to the courthouse and explained that he was in the hospital. This was one more "red flag" that Jeff was out of control and needed so much help. Later that week, Jeff called Susie to discuss options for his continued recovery before he was released. Susie reiterated the options to me, "Outpatient A.A. meetings or two weeks of rehabilitation." We all wanted at least a thirty-day inpatient, but two weeks seemed good at the time. Most facilities won't even take people who have attempted suicide until they have been in recovery for at least a month because they are such a high liability. One of the social workers suggested to me that I let him set up a tent in the backyard to live in.

On Friday, August 3, the hospital released Jeff to Saint Clare's rehabilitation center for fourteen days.

The following Friday, after a mere week there, Susie called and reported, "I participated in a conference call with Jeff and his alcohol counselor earlier this morning; Jeff had decided to check himself out of rehabilitation next Monday." This was not a good idea.

Sister Mary explained to Susie, "Jeffrey is doing well in the program, and no one can keep him here if he wants to leave. He wants to see his children, get a job, and get on with his life. He will be discharged Monday, August 6, unless he changes his mind."

There was nothing anyone could do to prevent this from happening. I was driving to pick Kelsey up from summer camp and wanted to explode. I went completely insane with fear and panic. I didn't have the energy anymore to fight with him. I wondered if he had the power to fight for himself.

That Monday morning, I saw my divorce lawyer and mentioned his release. She needed to protect me, Kevin, and Kelsey from Jeff's unannounced visits. She was also worried that he might try to harm me. We needed to keep him from tormenting me like he had before he attempted suicide. By early afternoon, I was in court with her, Jeff's lawyer, and a judge getting a restraining order prohibiting Jeff from entering the house until we figured out what turn his rehabilitation might take. No one knew what he would do next.

Early that evening, a car pulled beside me as I walked the dog up the street. It was Jeff. He looked ten years younger and appeared calm and rested. Other than his wrists being bandaged, he seemed normal.

I was frightened more than ever and only vaguely aware of the conversation. He asked, "Can I go into the house and use the phone? My cell isn't working?"

After spending the afternoon in court and thousands of dollars to prevent him from doing that, I said, "Go ahead."

For another moment, we continued to chat about the options he now had and delicately touched on the reality of what he faced.

I felt a strange combination of fear and guilt that remained lodged in my throat for months afterward. Disbelieving the overwhelming situation, I stood immobile for a few moments after he drove away. When I returned to the house twenty minutes later, he was gone. There was an envelope on the table on which Jeff had scribbled, "I'll be right back." My cell phone rang a moment later, and it was Jeff. He said, "Thank you for letting me use the phone."

I said, "Sure."

Although I didn't know it at the time, I would never see or talk to Jeff again.

This was his goodbye to me. I realized weeks later that when he went into the house that day, he had left the life insurance policies on his desk for me to find.

Chapter 17: Lost All Hope

What happens when you start to lose all hope? What happens when you wake up, day after day, without the faintest glimmer of light in your heart? When no matter where you turn to, all you find facing you is despondency and despair? Once you've buried yourself into a pit of misery and ache — how do you dig your way out of it? Or more importantly, how do you not let the sorrow engulf you completely? You can flail your arms around, but when you're drowning, what good are those meek and desperate movements? These are some of the questions that I asked myself when I found myself confronted with an unfathomable amount of pain and heartache.

In August 2007, my husband of twenty-three years lost all hope and committed suicide. Throughout the roller-coaster that had been our marriage, Jeff had struggled with alcoholism, depression, and his inner demons.

When your partner loses the will to live and sees nothing but a black void of despair consuming all happiness and joy, you begin to lose hope too. The year before Jeff's suicide, I had given up on us, and lost all hope for our life together, ultimately filing for divorce. There was no masking it— our lives were a constant struggle; me against him, and he against his powerful and insidious addiction. Now, I can't help but wince and turn away when I think of what he did in his desperation.

Although I could not save him—nor do I believe that it was my responsibility to save him — I can still tell his story to the world. For all the battles that he waged inside himself, my husband did try. When faced with the overwhelming power of his addiction, however, all his attempts were rendered futile. This, then, is the story of my husband's tragic path toward self-destruction and my subsequent recovery from years of emotional abuse and personal despair. In the end, it destroyed Jeff and quite nearly destroyed me too.

When I fell in love with Jeff, I thought it would be 'forever.' Love had come easily, and I spent more time with him, I found myself falling for him at an increasingly fast pace. Never did I think that it could turn so ugly, and be so difficult for so long. The beginning together is hard to recall, and the ending is impossible to forget. Jeff's addiction stole his life very slowly and subtly at first, until it was bigger than everything else. Addiction is a terminal disease, and people don't have to die from it; this is just a story of one man who did. Jeff's life became a constant struggle to survive and, in the end, suicide was his victory. Some people just can't be saved. Jeff tumbled into a dark pit of despair. There was no turning back as he suffered and destroyed his and our life. I was overcome with anger, confusion, and sadness for much of our life together. My heart physically hurt, and I cried for our innocent children being affected by this disease. I believed that our life together would be so complete and happy that he wouldn't need liquor anymore. I was wrong. Eventually, we didn't have the resiliency to face this challenge and stay strong as a couple.

He turned out to be one of those alcoholics who didn't have the capacity for the honesty needed to get better. Alcoholism defeated us, and we lost our equilibrium. Although I despised what he did, I feel it is crucial for me to defend his decision. I also forgave him. I simply would have paid too high of a price if I had refused. True forgiveness is letting go of all our ledgers of injustice and retribution and with open arms and remembering only the heart and goodness of the person that we loved. By the end, you barely recognize the person and the initial burst of love that you had felt dissipates into a hollow shell of what it used to be, but no matter how weakened, love never dies.

Talking about love, I remember the love that Jeff had for our children. The poet Anne Sexton wrote, "It's not who your father really was, it's who you remember him to be." Both our children had a natural tolerance and compassion for their dad. I know Jeff's love for them will remain in their hearts forever. I want them to remember the smart, funny, and talented father who loved them dearly and unconditionally, not the dad who was so desperately ill that he chose death instead of life. Kevin and Kelsey were the light of his life, his greatest accomplishment, his only pure joy in the darkness of his spiraling addiction.

My story is different but by no means unique. The devastation of alcohol addiction and suicide is played out within families all across the world. My hope is to reach out to those who have been through similar losses, to educate people about the ravages of this disease, and hopefully to provide some measure of support for those affected by both alcoholism and suicide. If my words can help even one person who is suffering, I will know that my efforts were not in vain. Addiction takes a toll, not only on the person who suffers from it, but to the loved ones around him. No one tells you what to do when you see the man you love spiraling into the depths of despair, and it can get quite lonely. By telling Jeff's story, I hope to tell others who might be in similar situations that they're not alone.

Chapter 18: The Healing

The nightmare of Jeff's addiction, D.U.I.s, legal and financial problems were over for him, but they were a horrendous beginning for me. As I began to shuffle through the mountains of medical forms, past-due bills, collection agency notices, and junk mail, the loss and ache of twenty-three years of his addiction began to consume me.

One minute, I felt guilty and sad; the next, I was angry. I had a hard time absorbing all that had happened. Jeff's life may have been a series of failures, but I never thought it would end like this.

That sweltering summer night, my husband, the love of my life, died from the love of his life: alcohol. I asked myself repeatedly, *"What could I have done differently?"*

After the excruciating horror of Jeff's suicide was over, the great weight of the days began. I was so distraught that, at times, I would have to pull over to the side of the road because I was crying so hard that I couldn't see. Other days, I couldn't let myself cry because I thought if I started, I would never stop. During countless grief-stricken nights, I sat up until dawn, fearing that my sanity was slipping away. I moved through my days in numb, slow motion, trying to keep some semblance of order at home for my children's adjustment to life without their father.

That fall, I spent my days obsessing over how Jeff could take his own life. Guiltily, I thought, why wasn't I able to stop him? Maybe if I had picked him up from the rehabilitation center that morning and helped him get settled in his apartment, I could have saved him. Maybe if I had been more tolerant of his alcoholism and remained in the marriage, he wouldn't have resorted to taking his life. The "maybes tormented me." Yet, over time, I realized Jeff had been determined to take his life no matter what I said or did to help him. There was nothing I could have done to change the outcome.

I thought back over the final months of Jeff's life, and again, feelings of remorse came back to haunt me. His first suicide attempt, his worsening alcoholism, his mounting debt, shrinking bank accounts, and major depression were huge red flags. Yet none of us knew just how fragile he was. He had been on the run for weeks, slipping away without anyone knowing what was happening. Sadly, I regret not trying harder to locate him or understand his pathetic state.

To answer my fault-finding questions about his suicide, I read many books I could on depression, bipolar disorder, alcoholism, and suicide. I talked to a grief counselor, joined a suicide survivors' group, and continued to educate myself on alcohol addiction. I discovered that suicide is not carried out exclusively by insane or mentally ill people, although who else would do this? I also learned that alcoholism does not discriminate. It affects people in all walks of life, from high-powered executives to skid row bums.

As I began to process these hard, cold facts, the puzzle pieces began to fit together. Things began to make sense, and my agony began to subside. I now know many factors influence a person's decision to commit suicide. The actual act is a release because it appears as a way to have balance and order in a dysfunctional life. People who commit suicide are trying to control their out-of-control lives. Death is just an act to end their unendurable pain. Jeff's mental anguish was so intense that it outweighed the physical pain of dying.

I could have spent my energy trying to understand Jeff's troubled soul to find more answers, but in the months after his death, I began to accept his suicide. I forgave him for what he had done. This forgiveness freed me to move beyond my pain. Today, I know he was an unwilling victim of the disease of alcoholism. It was never his choice to continue on such a destructive path. I now have compassion and empathy for all he endured.

Out of respect, I never said a bad word about Jeff to the children, especially after his death. Despite his indescribable pain, I know he wanted to be a good father and provider. As we recalled our good times with him, I always tried to accentuate Jeff's positive qualities.

I would go around telling them, "He loved you both very much He had a terrible disease, and he never meant to hurt you." Or, "Your dad was a good father; he was just having a mental breakdown."

By Thanksgiving of that year, I came to believe that the anguish of Jeff's addiction and the toll of his death would lift. My legal and financial issues were still unresolved, but I felt like I was beginning to rise back to the surface. I didn't cry nearly as much. I slept much better. I could go for long stretches without thinking about the horror of what I had just been through. I could even smile about some of our happy times as a family.

I had lunch with a friend who listened compassionately for years about my difficult partner. She heard me justify and defend staying in the marriage and plead to get out in the same sentence. I hear other voices of women who are confused between love and control. It's very slow and subtle, almost unnoticeable daily or even yearly.

Until one day, you realize something is wrong and that this is not what you want. Beyond a reasonable doubt, our lives had centered around Jeff's alcoholic behavior for the entire marriage. We were kept off-balance, even when things seemed steady and reliable. Jeff could devour tens of ketchup bottles in just a few seconds.

For the first time in over two decades, I was no longer controlled by Jeff's disease. I could focus on my own life and set a new path for my future. I can't believe I don't interact with anyone like that anymore. It's surreal to remain at peace throughout the day. No one is "furious" with me because I didn't pick up the milk. With every shred of reason, I wanted to understand and soothe, to pretend and minimize, so that the insanity didn't matter. I continuously balanced on a tightrope while keeping many balls in the air.

I think back to happier times, but I'm not nostalgic in a sad way. I was proud when Kevin was born, and Jeff whisked him off to change his diaper and play with him. I recall the laughter and hugs that we shared. I have many fond memories, and I don't want to forget them. I made plenty of mistakes, blamed myself for his sickness, and struggled with guilt, but I have survived.

The details of this whole journey that Jeff and I went through are becoming a bit blurry as the years go by. Searching for a balance, I can feel a sense of peace with Jeff's suicide. It's been an effort to stay afloat, not to drown in self-doubt, self-pity, and sorrow. I feel fortunate to have survived so much turmoil and despair with love and faith.

There is a thin line between remembering, focusing on, and living in that frame of mind enough to put down what I want to and move beyond the pain on paper. My mind wants to escape the trauma and forget, but I need to dwell a little longer in the trenches to tell my story. Was Jeff destined to die this way? Is even my greatest joy going to be tinged with a sense of sadness because of his death? These questions remain unanswered, and I hope to find their answers someday soon enough.

Chapter 19: By The Grace of God

The next few weeks and months of my life were inundated with the aftereffects of Jeff's life and death. I was bombarded with outstanding bills, creditors, collection agencies, phone calls and discoveries about what Jeff was doing before ending his life. I realized I didn't know him at all and just needed to gather more information to figure him out.

During the three weeks that we didn't hear from him he had been bouncing back and forth on a daily basis between south Jersey and north Jersey, staying in various hotels for a night here and a couple nights there. The Visa bill for $14,587 accounted for a few of these expenses but I never figured out how he spent that much money on. He had an apartment in Chatham near to the children to live in. It was discovered that he was withdrawing from his bank account multiple times a day. And he had cashed in another 401K for $29,000 in May and spent it along with unemployment checks, our joint checking account savings, and paychecks from his short period of employment. It is still a mystery what he spent all this money on.

While driving up and down the parkway every day he was blowing through E-Z pass without a tag. The state had pictures of the various cars and had sent him tickets which he ignored. I was technically still his wife and responsible for all his debt. I spent weeks sorting through the mess he intentionally left me with.

In September, I received a bill from Macy's cutlery department for $44.95. It was dated the day he was released from Saint Clare's rehabilitation hospital. I was livid and figured the store made a mistake. I mentioned this to a friend. She questioned, "Sandy, did Jeff have a Macy's credit card also?" In that instant, I realized what that meant. He had checked out of the hospital, driven to the mall, and selected the proper knife to murder himself with that night. And used the joint credit card to pay for it. It's amazing to me to think he had the presence of mind to carry out the mundane task of shopping for the right instrument to use. He had a definite premeditated plan. His decision hadn't been as impulsive as everyone thought. When I saw him on the street, he most likely had the knife with him and the plan to go to the hotel. The plan was in full swing. I can't even imagine how bleak a future could look to succumb to dying alone in a hotel bathtub.

Up until this time, I had thought Jeff had re-slit his wrists. After investigating what "acute exsanguination/air embolism" meant under "multiple stab wounds of abdomen" I knew what he did. I had never heard of anyone murdering themselves like this before.

I requested a copy of the autopsy report. I read the parts that I could decipher and felt like this was the ending I was looking for. It detailed multiple stab wounds of the abdomen, stab wounds of the liver, spleen, and small intestine with a butcher knife. The medical examiner noted Jeff was "late-middle-aged white male who appeared to be older than the stated age of 50 years." This surprised me since I had only seen him two days before and he looked young. The report described the incised wounds of both wrists, alcoholic liver cirrhosis, and stab wounds in the left and right abdomen cavity.

He had been sober.

As I cleaned through Jeff's bags and boxes with his possessions, I came across little mementos that reminded me who he was. There were hundreds of resumes sent out to businesses that showed the effort he made to find another job. Then nine tickets from two different police departments that showed his failure at ending his frightening addiction to alcohol. Did staring at his injured wrists remind Jeff that he had even failed at ending his life the first time? I don't pretend to know what he was thinking. I only saw the remnants of his nomadic life in my garage and wondered.

I came across material from the rehabilitation center. As illegible as his handwriting was, I could decipher the words, "plan-job, kids, stress, trigger points, etc." This was part of the outpatient recovery plan. For the last three weeks, the hospital had been vigilant in trying to assist him. No one knew the severity of his mental state, though, because his sanity act was so convincing. In between social workers, psychiatrists, doctors, and nurses treating him, I wonder if he had been planning his demise all along. His attempt was a very powerful indicator of his mental state of mind. Somehow, he knew how to conceal his intentions behind a non-suicidal facade. He wasn't willing to articulate his thoughts and plans, or else the hospital would have never released him. He displayed an agreeable, charming, and optimistic patient to the staff. He fooled even the best of them.

I found a 'sober for 24 hours" pin in his stash. I wished that he could have embraced all the AA program had to offer him- camaraderie, hope, faith, friends. But as his disease progressed, he became more and more isolated. The disease of addiction is profound and constantly invades the mental and spiritual souls of the people afflicted. He was in the throes of insanity, despair and addiction. He may have been hardwired for depression and anxiety. He was always weighed down by caustic, negative thoughts of his childhood. His troubling behavior became persistent and severe, all because of alcoholism. He had many symptoms of mental illness, bipolar disease, and cravings for alcohol.

Unfortunately, his alcoholism spanned decades. In the trenches of his addiction, Jeff's decision was not one sudden impulse, or even a single act. His final, self-inflicted death was a process that began months before he actually took his own life.

It was years ago, but I remember it clearly. The short-lived happiness we had: the hope when things were good; the love of our children, the way he looked at me the last time I saw him. He knew what to do. I knew nothing of who he had become. Maybe I never really knew who Jeff was. I barely knew who I was with him.

Grief changed the shape of my heart. All humans must cope with the death of loved ones but alcoholism and suicide layered my husband's death with guilt, betrayals, and recriminations that increased the pain for us. His death was as hard as his life. His bitterness was the last indignity of my divorcing him, while he drank away the retirement he had worked, saved and scrimped for, allowing me no peace.

I longed for love, forgiveness, understanding, and connection in those last few years, but the disease still held too much power over our family. In a perfect world, Jeff wouldn't have become an alcoholic, and I wouldn't have wanted to divorce him, and he wouldn't have died. I let go of the illusion of power over anyone but myself and moved into a more positive and productive direction. I moved towards hope. I had a lopsided view of life from living with the effects of this disease. One definition of insanity is "doing the same thing over and over again, expecting a different result." I did that for twenty-three years. Along the way, there were many awful, painful lessons to learn. It was excruciating to have to stand by and watch Jeff suffer every day of his life through depression, anxiety, and addiction. In so many ways, it was killing us both. Someone said it well, "Jeff may have taken his own life, but he saved Sandy's."

I no longer blame myself for his dying. I tried for 23 years to change this man and nothing I or anyone else did would make the outcome different. Jeff will live in our hearts forever. Deep down he was a wonderful person who suffered so much from the ravages of this terrible affliction. Somewhere along the way I had lost track of the separation between myself and Jeff.

I interceded for so long on his behalf—constantly reacting, worrying, pleasing, covering up, smoothing over, or bailing him out, that I had lost the sense of where I left off and he bagan. I was so enmeshed that I perceived myself as connected to him. I had no personal boundaries and confused this with love and caring. When I wrote the main story in this book fifteen years ago, it was just a grief journal.

After August 8th, 2007, I sat down at the computer every day and hammered out the years so I could figure out the puzzle of why and what happened. It all made perfect sense that Jeff would want to exit this life. Every day was a challenge for him just to wake up in the morning. No amount of love or money or security or help could have ever changed the outcome.

Every day for almost twenty-three years I fought for my sanity too. It was like I married Dr. Jekyll and out popped his alternative personality Mr. Hyde on a daily basis especially when he drank. I fought for my husband to be happy or at least content in his own skin too. That was virtually impossible given what I knew about his past. There was a lot unusual about his family of origin and childhood and up-bringing that could have predicted his anxiety, depression and addiction. He did suffer abuse and neglect. I don't know the details. It just seems relevant and does tell me something about his relationship with his father.

It's hard to believe my parents have been "gone " for 43 years. I've grappled with dealing with all the losses as any other person has. My friend says "I was born with a happy head". In other words, I am aware of inbred happiness, which although suppressed for many years due to childhood and marriage, I rose above to heal and rebound back to a natural happy and strong state of mind.

But only I know the many times I cried so hard while driving that I had to pull over to the side of the road. Or the hundreds of times I walked alone in the dark sobbing for the strength to understand and forgive a God that expects a child to grow up with this pain and loss. I spent a lifetime not fitting in and not feeling good enough. I still ask "why?" I still miss the mom I never got to know.

Every day I miss and pray to my mom for peace and patience. I'm sure my entire life would have turned out differently had she lived. I've missed a million moments with her unconditional love. It's easy to cry and be angry with God when so many other people have their parents. My grief has led to troubling behaviors through the many years of being lost.

My marriage was riddled with pain and confusion. But I am blessed with two of the best children in the world. So I thank Jeff from the bottom of my heart for them. I am lucky to have their unconditional love and support every day.

I didn't tell all the stories that I experienced with Jeff. Some, quite honestly, are too private to reveal and not really mine to tell. I just don't know how I survived sometimes. When I "feel the feelings' ' as they say in the twelve step programs, I go to a place where I honestly recall so much desperation, that I shy away. On any given day, the legacy I would like to leave my children with is the strength and perseverance to fight the demons that may haunt them. It's possible to forge a resilience to difficult times for generations to come.

I've heard the saying "Once I no longer need the lessons in life that unpleasant events offer me, I won't have events." I look at my own behavior as a chronic people-please, co-dependent, putting others' feelings and needs before mine until I lose my own voice until my own opinions seem to shrink. And the short quote "You can never get enough of what you don't want." I ask myself every day what I really want because eventually you just know it's never going to be any different. I stayed with Jeff when I really wanted to leave so I stayed halfheartedly. I was lukewarm with one foot out the door. He knew it and it wasn't fair to either one of us.

With writing this book, I hope that one person reads it and can relate to my story. Maybe they are in an unhappy relationship and petrified to leave. Maybe it'll help them see the way out of an abusive marriage or go into a program for themselves. I was brainwashed into believing I couldn't survive without my husband. I really wished I didn't have to go through the divorce by myself. It was easier to stay put but life's too short not to be a little happier. It's never easy either way but at least there is the chance things will work out. Or not... The past is preserved in memory, and the truth cannot be erased. I blame chance and destiny, not the man. Jeff needed one grain of luck, a seed of hope to grow into a reason to continue living. My choice now is to be happy and content. My children fill my journey with love and joy, now I am blessed as I travel through the rest of my life.

Made in the USA
Thornton, CO
11/12/22 10:28:16

bb9295e4-ac8d-483a-b1ab-12b87e8b501cR01